What actual readers and students have to say about A Tao of God…

I chose to seek endorsements from people who read pre-publication copies of *A Tao of God*; who have studied the principles and practices contained within it and used them in support of their own healing and spiritual evolution. **It is a very powerful work**, but then, read what actual readers and students have to say, for yourself… Ron McCray

Lynn Weaver, Leucadia, California:
Yes! Yes! Yes! … This book makes me want to jump for JOY! A MUST READ for anyone seeking the Truth of who we are… LOVE… thank you so much for sharing of yourself in such a loving way… this is certainly a keeper and that I would send as a gift to all I know and meet.

Alison M. Coppola, M.Ed.:
I've made more progress, emotionally and spiritually, in working diligently with the concepts in *A Tao of God*, than I have in the past seven years mastering several other metaphysical modalities. This book is a gem… it ties up the loose ends. It was my "missing piece."

Barbara Rose, author of If God Was Like Man, and Individual Power: Reclaiming Your Core, Your Truth, and Your Life:
A Tao of God is a timeless treasure. Whether you are highly evolved, or filled with doubts and insecurities, Ron McCray brings you wisdom and enlightenment that will forever help you to remember who you really are.

Sandra Sedgbeer, Author and Managing Editor, www.planetlightworker.com:
I am often asked to recommend books to people who are just beginning to awaken to their spirituality. Problem is, there's such a confusing and conflicting mass of information available, I've always considered it a difficult and daunting task to keep my list of recommended books to below 20 or 30 different titles.

What's needed, I have always felt, is a modern-day version of a "bible" – something that could not only be used like a roadmap or a guide to help an individual comprehend all the basics, but that could also reveal deeper layers of insights and new meanings as the reader's experience and understanding grows. For me, reading *A Tao of God* was like discovering several elusive works of art hiding within the pages of one deceptively slim volume.

I don't know how he did it, but Ron McCray has managed to distil all the essential principles, practices, knowledge and wisdom necessary to charting one's own unique course from spiritual confusion to spiritual enlightenment into less than 100 simple, straightforward, and blessedly easy to understand pages.

Based on McCray's own individual journey, beginning in 1991, the book reflects his own personal experiences and the fundamental truths (which I believe are relevant to all of us) that he uncovered along the way.

A must-read for the awakening beginner, as well as an excellent reference for those who have consciously traveled their paths for many years, *A Tao of God* is the kind of book you can return to over and over again, never failing to perceive something new and helpful on every occasion.

Margaret Fitzgearl, M.A .Curriculum and Instruction, California:
To read and study *A Tao of God* is to acquire knowledge of fundamental truths of life and ways of living that affect not only one's personal life but also overflow and become part of one's interaction in the workaday world. The messages presented are profound and reach the soul. *A Tao of God* is not a book to be read once and put aside. It is a book to refer back to again and again as one progresses through the ups and downs of daily life. Ron McCray has presented a true gift to the world as he courageously reveals his own evolutionary process, enabling others to benefit from his story and to proceed on their own paths.

Steve Wilson, Louisville, KY:
A Tao of God is a powerful and wonderful book that is deeply layered. It is like a new book every time I re-read it. Ron McCray's insights are essential for anybody on a quest of self discovery and healing. *A Tao of God* spoke to me on so many levels. I see it being a useful tool for anyone seeking to know more about themselves, whether they are just beginning the quest or well into the journey.

About Endorsements...

Please note this about most book endorsements. For most books, the majority of "back cover" endorsements is from famous writers or other well known people and appears as if the endorser actually read the book and wrote the endorsement. The reality is that the endorser rarely has read the book and agrees to have his or her name "attached" to an endorsement written by the author or a publicist. Authors do this as favors to one another. There is really no deceit intended in this practice, yet it does not give the potential reader of the book an honest appraisal of its merits.

A TAO OF GOD

Also by Ron McCray
The First Manager

A TAO OF GOD

**A "way" to heal the
pain and fear that shackle us**

Ron McCray

TURTLE WHEEL PRESS

TURTLE WHEEL SERVICES website: www.turtlewheel.com

Cover design by Damian Keenan: www.keenandesign.de

Printed in Victoria, Canada.

The principles and practices presented in this book should not be considered an exclusive method of confronting psychological and/or physical problems. It should be viewed as another resource to orthodox medical or psychological treatments.

National Library of Canada Cataloguing in Publication Data

McCray, Ron
    A tao of God : a "way" to heal the pain and fear that shackle us / Ron McCray.
ISBN 1-4120-0387-3
    I. Title.
BL624.M3964 2003   291.4   C2003-902818-6

TRAFFORD

This book was published *on-demand* in cooperation with Trafford Publishing. On-demand publishing is a unique process and service of making a book available for retail sale to the public taking advantage of on-demand manufacturing and Internet marketing. **On-demand publishing** includes promotions, retail sales, manufacturing, order fulfilment, accounting and collecting royalties on behalf of the author.

Suite 6E, 2333 Government St., Victoria, B.C. V8T 4P4, CANADA

Phone	250-383-6864	Toll-free	1-888-232-4444 (Canada & US)
Fax	250-383-6804	E-mail	sales@trafford.com
Web site	www.trafford.com	TRAFFORD PUBLISHING IS A DIVISION OF TRAFFORD HOLDINGS LTD.	

Trafford Catalogue #03-0756   www.trafford.com/robots/03-0756.html

10   9   8   7   6   5   4   3   2   1

Acknowledgments

It is often written in book acknowledgements, that there are far too many people to single out individually. This book is no exception for it is true. Literally, every person with whom I have (or have had) a relationship (and some that I simply observed or read) contributed in some small or large measure to *A Tao of God*. Here are some of the contributors whom I thank with great gratitude and appreciation, for they have touched my life in ways they will never know.

Kathy Boyce; Jack Broudy; Ken Carr; Lee Carroll; David Christal; Mike Congleton; Peter Conn; Alison Coppola; Dave Cox; Mark Daniels; Roy Dayton; Carol Edel; K. C. Ennis; Sean Faivret; Cindy Ferguson; Margaret Fitzgearl; Lance Giroux; Lee Grimes; Mildred Grimes; Robert Hamm; Steve Hansen; Linda Henning; Patricia Hirsch; Susan Hirsch; Catia Hirsch; Henry "Hank" Hirsch; Pamela Hollander; Sandra Holloway; Susan Holloway; Ronnie Hoy; Ron Hulnick; Mary Hulnick; Armella Jadali; Ed Klein; Dakota Sumi Lim; K-Sandra Love; Patrick Malone; Benjo Masilungan; Paul Mayberry; Patrick McCray; Susie McCray; Charles McCray; Susan McCray; Pam Milliken; Judith Morton; Lee Murphy; Ruben Neira; Dollie Nordmann; Janice Pavelco; Théo Parades; Steve Parker; Clare Peterson; Jack Rafferty; Susan Rosenstein; Steve Rother; Barbara Rother; Miguel Ruiz; Sandie Sedgbeer; Gemma Sedgbeer; Martin Shapiro; Bob Schick; Carol Schick; Ken Snyder; Rafael Vance Sparrow; Toni Torquato; Alberto Villoldo; David Whyte; Bob Whiton; Deborah Wilson; Steve Wilson; Brooke Wilson; Jay Wilson; Gary Zukav

Table of Contents

Dedication

To every person who seeks to know
himself or herself as a spiritual being.

Assumptions underlying my writing:

No one can ever give you that which
only you can **give** yourself.

No one can ever do for you that which
only you can **do** for yourself.

A Tao of God supports those who choose to
"give to and do for" themselves.

Ron McCray

The Well of Grief
By
David Whyte

Those who will not slip beneath
the still surface on the well of grief

turning downward through its black water
to the place we cannot breathe

will never know the source from which we drink,
the secret water, cold and clear,

nor find in the darkness glimmering
the small round coins
thrown by those who wished for something else.

Backward

Many books have a "Foreword" – an introduction to the actual book, a kind of where is the book headed "show and tell." I am writing this after completing *A Tao of God*, and I thought that looking back at the experience of writing the book could be of interest, hence a "Backward." If this view does not interest you (and that's OK), then I suggest you skip to the chapter entitled, Beginning.

A Tao of God did not begin as a book. I do spiritually based coaching, and although I have a model or approach for coaching, I had not written down how I go about it, and, in retrospect, I found that I would use different methods of starting the coaching process. Being a fairly left-brained person, my lack of consistency in initiating a coaching relationship with a client irked me somewhat, and on further reflection, I realized that, although the client and I usually ended up at the same place (the healing process), it took some people longer than others.

You could say that individual client differences account for the variation in time to get to the healing process, and I agree with you; however, there is another factor. Dare I call it the efficiency of the steps in getting to that important juncture in the coaching experience? Well, yes, I dare call it that. Efficiency and spiritual healing seem somewhat at odds with each other, but not really. Here's why.

I spent a lot of time and money dancing around in a circle seeking spiritual evolution or enlightenment. (I prefer "spiritual evolution" to "enlightenment" simply because the former infers a gradual progression, and the latter, a kind of binary state – either I am or I am not enlightened. Certainly my experience was/is one of gradual progression hence my bias in terminology.) The circle dance went on and on without me progressing beyond the dance floor. The dance was quite fun and exhilarating, yet, when the dance was over, the fun expended, and exhaustion set in, I wondered if I would ever really advance? The harmony and fulfillment that I sought in pursing matters spiritual was elusive. At times during the dance, I thought I "had gotten it" only to awaken to the cold, gray twilight of dawn with the realization that nothing had changed.

After pursuing years of personal growth and development programs and seminars, readings, group work, yoga, tai chi, being coached, books, crystals, numerology, fasting, journeys to sacred places, astrology, learning shamanism, energy healing, aromatherapy, candle gazing, meditation, and a formal study of spiritual psychology, I learned a lot and met many wonderful people, yet my life did not change. A life of harmony and fulfillment eluded me, a "will-o'-the-wisp" that danced in front me that I could not quite catch regardless of how long or hard I danced with it.

Finally, I figured out that where *I needed to go was inside of myself*, to the shadow places that are never illuminated by the Light – the places I did want to recognize as existing. *This was the place for healing*, not another weekend seminar in a conference center somewhere. I stepped into and illuminated my shadows. I healed my emotional wounds. Following that I began spiritual coaching. My goal was to take people inside themselves and support them in illuminating their shadows.

I knew that once I got someone to the point of choosing to make that inward journey, there was an excellent prognosis for healing. I experienced this over and over as a coach. The challenge became to devise a "way" to bring my client to that choice as quickly as possible. This was the origin of what became *A Tao of God*. The book not only contains the healing process, but it explains the entire set-up of being human. How does every one of us become emotionally wounded? What possible beneficial purpose do the wounds have? How can we heal them? How can we live life harmoniously and fulfilled after healing? How do we create what we truly need in life?

Looking backward, I see that I learned much in putting this book into print. I know too that my spiritual evolution never ends until I recycle myself and choose what's next as a spiritual being. I see life as drama and a comedy, though mostly comedy. Out of writing this book, I resolved to laugh more, listen more, and to be in the glorious moment as much as I can. I see that my life is truly about the journey, not the destination, for there is simply a succession of destinations; it is the quality of the journey that matters. I can tell you that continuing the journey after healing my wounds is to have harmony and fulfillment – at last.

May you be well and enjoy the journey of *A Tao of God*.

∞

Beginning

I realize that it may appear presumptive to write seemingly in the name of God. I get that. Please note however that this is *"A" Tao of God*, not "The" Tao of God. To say it is "The" Tao of God would be limiting and presumptive and not at all my intention. As described early on in this book, I believe that each of us is God, and that the Spirit of God exists not only in every human being but also in all things, animate and inanimate. This is a long-standing belief of shamanic traditions dating back tens of thousands of years. My experiences in the eleven years leading to writing this book validated the personal truth of this ancient belief.

The only requirements for you to find value in this book are to read it with an open mind and, if you are so inclined, try applying the principles and practices described herein. Although there is a linear sequence of sorts to the order of the 39 core chapters, the book is designed for reading randomly as well as sequentially. A mix of the two works well. I think it is a book you will find yourself coming back to periodically as the message of the chapters evolves as you evolve.

What is *A Tao of God*, and what's in it for you?

As to what's in it for you; if you are a "seeker;" if you are following the will-o'-the-wisp dancing in front of you just out of reach; if you yearn to be fulfilled and live in harmony, then there is value for you in *A Tao of God*. This work began with the awareness of needing to transform my own life. At the outset, the challenge looked enormous. I walked through my life in a rut much like the entrenched path of an ox slowly hauling the weight of his life around in a circle for years. I had no idea how to begin. It was to be the greatest and most challenging adventure in my life… so far.

A Tao of God is what happened to me along my "way." I make no apologies for it, and I also admit that it came to me in various ways over a period of eleven years. Some of the knowledge contains concepts and principles that are very old, and some of the knowledge came to me directly in a variety of settings and methods, a combination of sources and Source. *A Tao of God* describes how I climbed out of the deep rut that was my life and freed myself from the burdens I had dragged around for over 50 years.

Tao is an ancient Chinese word that roughly translates as "way." *A Tao of God* is the path that I follow in spiritually evolving. I use the present tense of "follow" in the sense that I am still evolving, and believe I will continue evolving until I die. Each of our paths is different and also similar. Discernment is the ability to take what each of us specifically needs and leave the rest behind. That is my invitation to you: take what appeals to you from the "way" of my path and use it howsoever you wish in traveling your own path. I wish you well.

The model for all manner of "Tao" (pronounced "dow") books is the Tao te Ching, an ancient book (circa 600 BCE) written by an obscure Chinese hermit and monk, Lao Tsu, who is thought to predate Confucius. It loosely translates to "Book of the Way." It consists of 81 chapters, each one only a few lines in length. There are many translations and applications of the original Chinese (an ancient dialect that can no longer be literally interpreted).

The Tao te Ching is very esoteric and vague. Each chapter can be interpreted many ways and is rarely definitive in its meaning. Part of its fascination is in musing about what it really means. *A Tao of God* does not attempt to interpret or parallel the Tao te Ching. My "way" has 39 chapters and deals straightforwardly with what I learned on my spiritual path.

The chapters, or steps, of A Tao of God are an integral part of my interpretation of Life Mastery based on a four-step transformation model:

Knowledge➜ Experience➜ Understanding➜ Transformation

Reading the contents of A Tao of God represents the Knowledge step. The Experience step consists of putting that Knowledge into action. The result of being in action is a unique grasp of the Knowledge that is mine and mine alone. I call this step an "Understanding," and it is unparalleled. No one else can have my precise Understanding, nor can I have theirs. Completing this third step placed me at a crossroad. Knowledge was gained and its Experience resulted in a one-of-a-kind, personal Understanding that I could continue to apply and use, or not – my choice. Choosing to take the fourth step is what made a difference in my life.

Step four, Transformation, occurred from the repeated application of an Understanding until I reached the highest level of learning, unconscious competence: being and doing without thinking. To get to that level, I used awareness and commitment to continuously apply the Understanding to my life until I no longer needed to think about it. It became automatic. This was Transformation. There were many parts of my life and my way of thinking that needed Transforming. Transformation is the payoff of A Tao of God, and it is what enabled me to create harmony and fulfillment in my life, and it can do the same for you as well. Remember, Transformation always begins with Knowledge.

My human "wiring" causes me to see the world in terms of dualities: I see night and day, experience hot and cold, look up or down, and judge events and people as good or evil, ugly or beautiful, rich or poor, stupid or smart, capable or incompetent, and so forth. In effect, I hold a bag of two-sided, "duality" coins, and I am continually reaching in the bag, pulling out a coin, and reacting according to which side is up. Is it good or evil, right or wrong, and so on, depending on the nature of the coin? The subtle irony is that since both sides belong to **the same** coin, there is, in fact, no duality, and so, how can one coin be both good <u>and</u> evil?

The coin is the same regardless of which side is up. The other side is not visible but is there nonetheless. It exists and can be turned up in a heartbeat. Same coin, two sides. Please bear this in mind as you read this book. You will often be pulled by the illusion of duality to "choose" one side over the other. Please remember that it is an illusion. Duality is discussed further in chapter 21 within the context of karma.

Remember one essential "truth" as you read *A Tao of God*:
Spiritual evolution is simple but not easy.
When you examine any "system or "process" for healing and evolving yourself including *A Tao of God*, if it does not seem simple, it is not for you.

My evolution is a matter of "collapsing" the two sides of the "duality" coins into the unity of all things.

∞

The Origin of Self

Chapter 1 – Who am I?

"Who am I?" is the first of three, self-defining questions that can be answered countless ways. How I see myself is a wonderful way to gauge where I am in my spiritual journey, even when I am not aware of being on such a journey.

There are four dimensions by which I can measure who I am. All are always in play even without the consciousness of what they are.

The first is physical. My physical body demands much of my time simply to keep it in good enough condition to maintain life. Survival is paramount here. My body must have air, water, food, shelter, and clothing (or some way to regulate body temperature). It is possible to define myself largely by this dimension especially if survival is tantamount in the moment. All of us define ourselves physically some of the time.

The second is mental. Man is capable of rational and analytic thought. Man not only learns (and most creatures can learn to some degree), he can also synthesize information, i.e., combine A with B and get something new, C. Many people on the Earth today define themselves in terms of how and what they think. All of us define ourselves mentally some of the time.

The third dimension is emotional. Emotions are difficult to pin down, for they are the product of mental activity as well as physical events, yet they are neither rational nor can they be expressed except as learned labels such as happy, sad, frustrated, angry, and so on. Some people define themselves emotionally most of the time. All of us define ourselves emotionally some of the time.

The fourth dimension, which is independent of the other three, is spiritual. Spiritual is variously defined; for my purpose, it is my belief in something greater than myself of which I am a part. The spiritual is reflected in religion, philosophy, and other belief systems. For some people, spirituality is the rote conduct of rituals and practices with little awareness of a higher order of being. For others, spirituality is consciously seeking and connecting with a higher order of being. All of us define ourselves spiritually at some time.

There is also an overlay of time with any and all of these four dimensions, so we can use one measurement now, and another measurement later. This game of life is great fun, so loosen up your laugh muscles and prepare to amuse yourself as you explore the who, the why, and the what of human beings.

I am nothing, and I am everything.

∞

Chapter 2 – Where did I come from?

"Where did I come from?" is the second of the three open-ended, self-defining questions. Timelines often characterize answers to this question. "Where did I come from?" for many people is a function of where they were when.

Many people answer this question from the perspective of physical origin, and it is accurate to say that to some degree we reflect where we live or lived. Even though people may live in places not of their origin, when asked, "Where are you from?" their replies are not where they live now, but where they spent their childhoods, their concept of home.

What is home and where is it really? Am I a spiritual being having a human experience? Or when I die, is there only a great void into which I am thrown without further conscious existence? The answers to these questions helped me form my response to, "Where did I come from?"

Perhaps I want there to be a hereafter that assumes a "herebefore" as well. Why not? Thinking about the veil and an existence beyond is just thinking about it. What does it take to have the realization that I am immortal, not as a human but as an aware consciousness?

It took my willingness to look where I could not see. The first aware steps on my path were taken in darkness. Doing so required resolve, courage, and a need to believe there was something more powerful than the fear that kept me in the dark.

I have always been, and where I came from is the place to which I am returning.

∞

Chapter 3 – Why am I here?

"Why am I here?" is the third and last of the self-defining questions. This question is perhaps the most revealing of the three. Confronting my reason for being is not something that was easily undertaken. To express why I am here involves looking deeply into my life up to this time as well as into the broader view of what lies unfinished before me, perhaps not even begun.

I live day-to-day, meeting and dealing with the challenges of living using the tools and skills I have learned. Each day is predictable and also unknown. Each day bounces through the corridors of life between the wall of the mundane and the wall of controlled terror - all of that without knowing why I am here.

Looking at this question can raise thoughts of inadequacy, of failure, of dreams unfulfilled; or I can float above those considerations and search for the grander purpose of my life, knowing my search will always yield a true answer.

I am here to love myself unconditionally, and in so doing, love the universe and everything within it.

∞

Chapter 4 – God

*A belief in God is mandatory for me to make sense of my life.
God is the part of the puzzle of life that brings focus to
everything. Nothing makes sense to me without God.*

By the very nature of how I define "spiritual," it stands to
reason that the existence of God is a personal truth for me.
"Personal" in the sense that my concept is my concept, and in
no way do I presume it is what everyone is to believe or hold
as true.

Whether or not there is a God is a debate ranging over
thousands of years. There is no definitive answer – on either
side. For me there is no longer a debate, although for the first
half century of my life I did not believe in God. Now, my
assuredness in the existence of God is a given. The
experiences I had over the last ten plus years removed all
doubt about the existence of a greater consciousness than my
own. From physical sensations, such as becoming virtually
paralyzed by energy rushing through my body to visions
(vividly experiencing my own death), I am repeatedly and
frequently made aware that there is more to my life and living
than my human body and mind.

**God therefore is at the center of *A Tao of God*, and from that
center, all things are understandable.**

My presence on the Earth, and that which makes me human,
is based on the existence of God. To receive value, *A Tao of
God* requires a belief in God. Moreover, receiving value from
A Tao of God requires examination of these specific beliefs:
- God is love.
- God is the beginning and end of all things, the
  "Collective" of all that is.
- God is energy of the highest vibration.
- God is without judgment.
- God is contained within everything, especially
  humans.

My access to God is through my Higher Self. What's that? My Higher Self is my portal through the veil of opacity my three dimensional existence as a human being imposes upon me. It is actually not there, but because I *believe* it is there, it is. In my human skin suit, my only access beyond the third dimension is through my Higher Self. My Higher Self is part of the entire package of me as a spiritual entity: mental, physical, and emotional (the three human bodies stuck in three dimensional reality), and spiritual (Higher Self and Soul) that transcend the three dimensions.

When I am *aware*, I can invoke my Higher Self who dwells in the fourth dimension and gain access to the fifth dimension, a classroom to which different aspects of God Source visit me so that I may gain knowledge and manifest what I need for my human existence. My Higher Self is the conduit for me to the rest of Source, God, the Universal Collective – there are many names. I am simply going to use "God."

I am God, so are you, and we are love.

∞

Chapter 5 – There was no cosmic mirror...

*Why human beings? This reflects the, "Why am I here?"
question. Imagine that you have lived forever in a vast land
that has no end and also has nothing that reflects your image.
Imagine also that you are immortal. You can see everything
around you but you cannot see yourself. Would you not be
curious?*

God was curious about the nature of Itself but could not "see"
Itself. I cannot know the nature of something unless I have a
contrast to that something. I cannot know light except for
having experienced the dark. A fish lives in water and
therefore does not know "not water." It can pass its entire life
never being aware of water. But, remove the fish from the
water and it is suddenly and painfully aware of "not water."
The distinction is strongly created by the contrast.

God could not distinguish Itself for there was no contrast. God
is everything and everywhere. How could God distinguish
Itself?

Contrast creates distinction for God and me

∞

Wounding: The Genesis of the Shadow Self

Chapter 6 – The design

*The dilemma God faced is that God could not experience
Itself as there was no contrast to Itself. Since God is
everything, how could a contrast be created? The solution was
brilliant (not surprising). The solution was human beings. The
design of the human experiment is God's solution to knowing
Itself. Here is the way it works. Since God is everything, so we
too must be God. So what's different? In the process of birth
(materialization limited to the third dimension), God "veiled"
us from the awareness that we **are** God. We are born into an
existence in which we perceive that we are less than what we
are and quickly learn that we are not automatically blessed
with unconditional love. The creation of the illusion of not-
love gives God the contrast that enables It to know Itself.
There is more…*

There are rewards to playing the game of life. If I can find a
way to remember who I really am and learn to love myself
unconditionally, I can create heaven on Earth until I return to
the other side of the veil. This is the highest message of *A Tao
of God*.

Here are my rules to the game of life:
- I am a physically mortal being unaware that I am
  divine and immortal because of "the veil."
- I have a physical shell that continuously demands
  attention and diverts me from gaining the awareness
  of my divinity.
- As I play out my life, my unawareness that I am God
  allows God to experience Itself until such time (and if)
  I reconnect with my own divinity through
  unconditional self-love.
- My goal in life is to reconnect with God and to
  remember who I truly am, thereby proving that the
  power of unconditional self-love is so compelling it
  can eventually surface into human experience.
- I can then create heaven on Earth.
- I am not penalized or judged by God for what I do or
  don't do.

- I cannot lose.
- I can re-enter the game multiple times.

I am committed to having the awareness that I am God, and as is everyone and everything else.

∞

Chapter 7 – Choice and consequences

To make the design complete, God gave humans a gift, the gift of choice and free will. Thus I know that reconnection with God is a choice, not a condition. Each day, I am presented with many choices, and the choices I make determine my progress in remembering who I am. There are many competing choices – many of them are labeled as "Satan" or "evil." To be sure they exist but only in my mind.

Every conscious action I take is a choice. Each choice presented to me has one or more consequences associated with it. I may turn left or I may turn right – each choice has a different outcome. There is no divine intervention, including suggestions as to which choices I make. In my seemingly detached state from God, I must choose, and in so doing, accept the consequences of my choices.

As a human, I experience a vague, indefinable aloneness for I am veiled from knowing that I am God and thus connected to the Universe. Reconnecting is the passion that sits on my right shoulder nudging me towards something that I can only barely discern if at all.

Each time I choose an action not based in love, I know that I will be presented with more choices to express love, to be love. Some call this karma.

My experience… Through much of my life, I believed that there were certain aspects of my life that were rigid and could not be changed. For example, I mistrusted authority. I did not like anyone telling me what to do. You can imagine how well that went over in my four years of sea duty as a naval officer! As a consequence, although not a rebel (that was too overt for me), I had a lot of passive-aggressive conflicts with superiors, and in fact, worked subversively (but not effectively) to undermine their authority and often got found out – more trouble. The dynamics of karma kept putting "authority figure" conflicts in my face until I finally leaned to lovingly accept those who had some authority over me. It was not easy but was a necessary step along my evolutionary path.

In my awareness of God's design, I will strive to reconnect spiritually in the face of compelling human pressures to define myself physically, mentally, and emotionally.

I am responsible for my choices and their consequences, for I am a part of all things.

∞

Chapter 8 – Primal abandonment

Primal abandonment occurred when I discovered that the divine love with which I was born had a contrast: "not love." With that realization, the veil dropped, and my connection with God was seemingly severed. I know now when it happened, although I did not know at the time – I was six years into this life.

No matter how benign or loving were the adults in my early years, primal abandonment had to occur, for it was necessary to drop the veil so that I "forget" who I am. God became an omnipotent abstract, unknowable and unreachable, for a small child sitting in a large pew of a church, while all the time, I **was** God. What a great cosmic farce!

As a result of primal abandonment, I learned that "not love" exists. What I made of this was that love is not my birthright; it is conditional and must be earned. That's when I came to know danger and fear, two powerful emotions that would shape my life for decades. Even now, after having learned the mysteries revealed here in *A Tao of God* they still shadow me wherever I go.

This is the fall from grace in the Garden of Eden. This is the cross that Christ bore upon Golgotha. This is all the fables and allegories of how man was cast out by God. I know now that neither I nor anyone else was cast out. We are of God, and by agreement, we all play in this game of remembering who We are.

Primal abandonment is necessary to the game, the experiment. Can I remember my divinity? Do I have one life or many to accomplish reconnection? Nothing is predetermined, and the outcome for me is immaterial, for it is how I play the game while in this energetic form that counts.

I think it helps to remember that my life is a game. That I do not always see life as a game is, at its core, funny. The humor comes from my "seriousness" about being a human, running around in my skin suit, overly concerned with the trappings of being human, which I regard as "significant," when in fact they have no more significance to my spiritual self than a movie or television show.

Someone once described life to me as a great improvisational play in which I have my story line, as do many others with whom I will interact in the acts and scenes of our lives. We stay true to our characters, yet, because of free will and choice, we improvise our way through life. Comedy and drama are all the same at the curtain call. Remember to laugh.

My experience… When I was six, I "played" at being my father (who was a mechanic) and got filthy dirty in a grease pit. To my young mind, I was only doing what my father did every day, and surely my mother and he would be very proud of me. That was not the case, as my mother became enraged when she saw me and later my father beat me for what I had done. The principle of "not love" became abundantly and painfully clear. I then resolved to learn the rules and play by them to avoid punishment and hopefully "earn" love. This was primal abandonment. Its "lessons" shaped my life for decades.

My primal abandonment is a blessing, for it is my ticket of admittance to this theatrical performance, which is this grand game of life on Earth.

∞

Chapter 9 – Strategies and tactics

Strategies and tactics result from primal abandonment. They are how I learned to cope with "not love." I learned them early, sharpening and refining them as I grew into an adult. Some of them enabled me to be successful in human endeavors; others resulted in the experience of deep grief and unhappiness – consequences of my choices to use my strategies and tactics.

Strategies and tactics are about surviving in a world apparently filled with not-love. If I believe that love is conditional and that it must be earned, then the effectiveness of my strategies and tactics measures my success as a human being but not as a spiritual being. Survival from all perceived threats, physical and psychological, is hardwired into my human package.

Survival strategies are basic ways of being that are reflected in my life's themes. One of them is my choice to avoid being seen – to be invisible. When I am invisible, I cannot be blamed for inappropriate actions. As a strategy or theme my invisibility enabled me to avoid "not love" by staying below the threshold of notice: out of sight, out of mind. My invisibility strategy came into play in many situations: school, home, social situations (at gatherings I learned to be transparent), and later in life, business and the military.

Survival tactics are the maneuvers that I used within a strategy to deal with specific situations. A tactic for invisibility is to dress conservatively, remain at the back of the room, and to rarely speak out or engage in as little conversation as possible. My tactics became more efficient and effective as I aged. My strategies remained much the same, serving as fundamental ways of moving through life.

I have two different types of survival strategies and tactics. The first is defensive and prevents people from noticing that I am only conditionally lovable – that I am unworthy of unconditional love. The second is offensive and is used when I suspect that someone is on to my conditional lovability. I have been found out and must divert his attention away from my unworthiness by being angry, belligerent, and hostile.

My personal mantra reflected my core strategies:
"Don't screw up, make waves, or get caught."
This is how I lived until I began to awaken.

∞

Chapter 10 – Needs, wants, wishes, and desires

Need versus want, wish, and desire is crucial in understanding how I came to be where I am. The distinction is necessary to taking the first step in rediscovering self-love.

First, let's examine needs.

What is a need? I do not have very many needs. At the most fundamental, I need air, water, food, fire, and shelter. These are elements of the Earth that sustain my life so that I may seek to fulfill higher needs. The brilliant 20th century psychologist, Abraham Maslow, postulated a hierarchy of need having five levels:

1. Survival,
2. Social,
3. Esteem,
4. Love,
5. Self-actualization ("enlightenment").

The identification of these five levels of need is somewhat obvious. The greater contribution made by Maslow was in pointing out that the needs at one level must be met before someone can move to the next level. For example, if a person does not have his "survival" level needs (air, water, food, shelter) met, he will not focus on "social" level needs (community, occupation, education, law). The implication of this principal to spiritual evolution is that a person is not going to be ready to fulfill spiritual needs (level five) until the four lower level needs are met.

The wounds from primal abandonment result in blockages at the love and esteem levels. Many people, at one of these two levels, sense that they are blocked, yet do not realize that the blockages result from primal abandonment; hence, they are not open to undertake the emotional healing to clear the blockages. Instead, they look for ways outside of themselves to move forward and instead end up moving in a circle. Some people stay in this circular movement for years or decades; some people pass from life without exiting it.

My experience... I know this circular movement well for I "circled" for decades. In my twenties I restlessly sought "something" in my life that I could not pin down. I was solidly entrenched at the social level of Maslow's hierarchy. I read metaphysical books, sat under trees contemplating the nature of my life, and rigorously practiced yoga for several years, yet the inner peace I sought, eluded me. I "circled" in my home at the time, Louisville, until I moved to San Diego in my mid-40's. I did not stop circling when I reached California, and the circle got bigger.

For a seeker, southern California is a mecca. There are so many metaphysical and spiritual goodies to sample. In Louisville I discovered the Tao te Ching and *Autobiography of a Yogi* by Paramahansa Yogananda. In San Diego, I began the practice of tai chi and could actually visit the Self-realization Fellowship begun by Yogananda. Moreover, there were bookstores, societies, readings, new age shops, an array of energy healers, astrologists, numerologists, channelers, coaches and gurus, seminars, retreats, and classes. What to do first?

I partook of a lot of these goodies, learned a lot, met many wonderful people, and yet, harmony and fulfillment eluded me. I was circling, not moving forward. I was not yet awake. I did not even know about primal abandonment. Like so many others, I continued to seek but outside of **me**, while the true need for healing lay inside me, out of sight. Pursuing my "higher" needs would move me along my individual "way" of Spiritual evolution by transforming more and more of my life to be aware of being God. But how did I know what they were?

Slowly, I realized that fulfilling a need eases my yearning TO BE MORE, not HAVE MORE, and then I began separating needs from wants, wishes, and desires.

How do I tell the difference between a need, and a wish, want, and desire? Satisfying a need moves me closer to heaven on Earth. Desires hold me Earth bound. The Earth is a wondrous place that we are given on which to stage the play of life; it is not the final destination. The Earth is an entity to be thanked for what She provides for the support of my humanness, and as such, deserves my respect and care. Although my flesh may be released back into the Earth, it is not the domain of spirit. Heaven on Earth is created by having my needs met.

How do I determine my needs? A need presents a doorway to fulfillment. A need involves other people rather than just the self. A need is a contribution; it is a giving, not a taking. A need speaks to the highest expression of my being. A need is about being God, not playing God. Where is my life focused in each moment: on need or desire?

How do I know if I have everything I need? When I have everything I need, I am fulfilled, harmonious, content, and joyful. Each of us has different needs, for they define our individual "ways" on the Earth. Finding and satisfying my needs is a crucial part of my life's work.

Do I obsess to possess?

If my life is about acquiring the material, the powerful, the political, the "visual," then I may be obsessive about possessing, and that's okay for it is my choice with its attendant consequences. If so, I know that inside of me are needs that wait patiently for recognition and fulfillment. I can always go to that place. It is never "too late."

Fulfilling a need completes me, while satisfying a desire results in more desire.

∞

Chapter 11 – Dissatisfaction with life

The starting point for my journey within to unconceal and heal my dark or shadow side began with realizing that I would have life be other than what it is. To have my life be different than what I was experiencing involved change. There are two kinds of change. One is change based in desire; the other is based in need. There is a big difference between the two.

The effects of primal abandonment created a dark or shadow side in my emotional and mental bodies that my ego does not want to be available to my consciousness. Ego hides these areas (and their precipitating events of learning that love is conditional) in favor of the strategies and tactics that I created to protect myself. I trade "apparent" safety provided by my ego for peace of mind.

The tug of war between my ego's strategies and tactics designed to protect me from being judged unworthy and my need to spiritually evolve is the crux of emotional healing. I cannot emotionally heal **and** keep my ego-based strategies and tactics intact. There are many definitions and explanations of the origin of the ego. The one that I use here is not meant to invalidate any others; my definition is for the purpose of creating the perspective in which emotional healing is accomplished. With that in mind, my concept of ego's origin is that ego is created at the moment primal abandonment is experienced.

Recall that in that moment, I experienced the illusion of the duality of "love and not love." Since my prime spiritual directive as a human being is to live in a state of love, and suddenly I discover there is a "not love," then I must create a mechanism that works to make me lovable as much of the time as I can. This mechanism is full of behaviors, thoughts, and judgments, all designed to keep me safe from experiencing "not love." I call it ego. I believe that if one person lived an entire life time in a perpetual state of love, he or she would have no ego.

The ego is largely a creation of the emotional body with a supporting role played by the mental body. Emotion ranks "higher" in the human hierarchy than intellect; therefore, the emotional body sets up requirements for the intellect to satisfy. "Higher in the hierarchy" means which body gets precedence. The hierarchy from top to bottom is: physical, emotional, mental, and then spiritual (Higher Self and Soul). This is not in order of importance, but simply in the order of where does my attention go first? If I stub my toe, the reaction is physical, not emotional (that comes later – why was I dumb enough to stub my toe?), and certainly not mental or spiritual.

Given that the experience of primal abandonment is initially emotional, it is reasonable that my mental body steps forward to assist my emotional body in the creation of the ego as a set of defensive and offensive strategies and tactics that serve to protect me from "not love."

There remains, however, the *need* to fully and unconditionally love myself. This need is "hard wired" into my being. I came into the world with it, and it never goes away. The condition of not loving myself creates dissatisfaction with my life that shows up repeatedly. It may express itself in my relationships, occupation, health, or other unique ways.

Heraclitus, a Greek philosopher who lived circa 500 BCE, coined the expression, "Change is inevitable," and so it is because humans must have change to survive. The question becomes: What kind of change? If I seek an *ego-based* change because of a want, wish, or desire, the change will not lead to harmony and fulfillment, but to desiring even more change. If I seek change to meet a need that enables my spiritual evolution, then I will experience harmony and fulfillment, and within the domain of the change, I am satisfied.

True spiritual dissatisfaction comes from *needing* life to be different than what it is. This "need" caused me to begin the process of learning to love myself fully and unconditionally. The journey to find self-love began with the *awareness* of my need for my life to be different.

My experience... When did this awareness first occur for me? I sat in a hotel meeting room in 1991 attending my first personal growth and development seminar. In the third day of the four day seminar, I experienced an epiphany, and it was not a happy one. While participating in a game on that third day, I finally became *aware* that I wanted to see other people fail. I saw that my "failure fetish" showed up in every aspect of my life that involved other people.

It was such a powerful, ego-based strategy that I had sacrificed marriage, friendship, and professional success to it. Being aware that it existed and understanding its power over me, I then had the beginning point of my journey, namely that I could change who I was being – that I could find the harmony and fulfillment that I sought for so long. There would be many years, tears, and jeers until I discovered that I must emotionally heal in order to live a life of harmony and fulfillment, but I was resolved to do so, and thus it began.

Now, I know that my life is measured in moments, and each moment is an opportunity, actually a choice, to experience either love or fear. Fear is the "typical" state for most people most of the time. Fear is learned; love is part of the human package – it just gets submerged in fear. Understanding that unconditional self-love is my birthright is to begin understanding how to choose love over fear.

When I articulated my need for life changes, my first step on the journey to self-love was taken.

The need to change my life was the motivation to spiritually evolve.

∞

Chapter 12 – Judgment

Judgment is a two-sided "duality" coin that I carry with me everywhere. Judgment is the end product of practicing survival strategies and tactics. It is my shorthand for knowing whether I am in offensive mode (attacking others to divert them from discovering that I am not lovable) or defensive mode (demonstrating my lovability by being what others want me to be).

The two sides of the judgment coin are inferior and superior. It is the same coin. If one side is down then the other is up – still the same coin – it is just that one side is hidden. If the superior side is up, I engage in "I am superior" strategies and tactics by overpowering those who may be on the verge of discovering that I really am not lovable (or so I think). Superiority strategies and tactics include anger, aggression, condescension, silence, arguments, withholding affection and friendship, aloofness, attacks (physical or psychological), and so on.

If the inferior side is up, I use "I am inferior" strategies and tactics to prove that I really am lovable. I will do what it takes to gain recognition and acknowledgment. "I really want to earn your love, please!" Inferiority strategies and tactics occur as pretense, fawning, lying, laughing at jokes I don't find funny, agreeing with someone when I really don't, yielding to "group think," not expressing how I feel or what works for me, trying to impress, attempting to be someone I am not, and so on.

As in all applications of duality, the two sides are illusions. There is no inferior, nor is there superior. Both are judgments created by humanity, not the design of God. All divine energy is the same; there are no variations. Love is love, end of discussion.

The sum total of my judgments is my ego. Ego is the general in my war to win the love of others. Sometimes my ego appears inferior and becomes defensive; sometimes it is superior and takes the offensive, but winning the war is always the objective, although I can never really win. How can I win over something that is an illusion? The famous cartoonist, Walt Kelly, wrote this immortal line for his character, Pogo Possum, "We have met the enemy and he is us." The dynamics of my ego can be understood by observing my judgments since, because of them, I am surely my own worst enemy.

My experience... I could fill an encyclopedia with my judgments (and those are only the ones that I remember). However, I will spare you that, and just relate one very large one that followed me around like gum stuck to my shoe. I judged most of the people for whom I worked during my career in corporate America as not having enough sense to walk in out of the rain. I, of course, did have enough sense to do so with a lot left over. I was constantly critical of these people, privately and publicly. As you might imagine, I lost several jobs because of my judgment. My judgment was rooted in my fear that I was not good enough, so I attempted to shift attention to the unworthiness of those for whom I worked. It was not a very successful strategy, but persisted until I became aware of what I did, and then I transformed my judgment into loving acceptance – what a difference.

I am not my ego, but for a long time, I thought I was.

∞

Chapter 13 - Fear

Scratch a judgment and find a fear. My prime directive as a human is to avoid harm. (Unconditionally loving myself is the prime directive of my spiritual body.) I must avoid harm to my body in order to continue living. I also learned to use my survival strategies and tactics to avoid psychological harm.

The measure of successfully avoiding physical harm is easy to gauge: am I alive and functioning or not? The measure of successfully avoiding psychological harm (being unloved or found unworthy of love) is not so easy. I am not much concerned with physical survival, but psychological threats abound in day-to-day life. Because I often don't know the outcome of a psychological threat, I make up what I don't know. That is fear.

A threat is real. Fear is not. When I hear footfalls behind me in a dark alley at night, a potential threat exists. When I begin making up what I don't know about the footfalls, I create fear.

When fear is present, I have three classic, ego-based strategies to employ:
- I can flee – an inferiority strategy.
- I can fight – a superiority strategy.
- I can flounder, stuck in place – an inferiority strategy.

None of these strategies releases fear; they merely ease the grip of fear for a while.

Fear is counter-productive. It robs me of energy and reason. It is physically and emotionally debilitating. Fear prevents me from recognizing and meeting my needs.

My experience… my fears were many and ran the gamut of human experience. One of the greatest ones was my fear of abandonment by women. As an adult, whenever I entered into an intimate relationship with a woman, I started counting down the time until she left me. For a while, I insulated myself and resolved to leave her before she left me. That way I was in control. As I got older, I wanted to remain in a relationship, and guess what? I created her leaving me anyway, so my old self-fulfilling prophecy of abandonment did indeed come true. Such is the power of a deeply rooted fear – my belief in my fear became real because I unconsciously manifested it. Now, that is "scary."

I live my life, consciously or unconsciously choosing, moment by moment, to be in the state of fear or the state of love.

∞

Healing: Finding Self-love

Chapter 14 – Fact versus fear fiction

*What I don't know about a threat, I make up, and thus create fear. It is what I call a story. My story is composed of facts and fear fiction. Fear fiction gets created when I believe that I am **potentially** at risk of being harmed.*

Each of my stories has a beginning, middle, and an end. Moreover, each story has a "point" or a theme, and so, what is the story about? The story's point is the clue to discerning the story's fear fiction component. I put my story into words with the beginning, middle, and end, and then I ask myself the question, "What is the theme, what is this story about?" The answer is my fear fiction.

Here are some stories…

- "Sure, I could ask Mary to go on a date, but there is no use in asking; she won't go."
- "The way things are going, I am sure to lose my job and end up loosing everything."
- "There has been a lot of cancer in my family, I know I will eventually get it and die."
- "I should have never loaned my brother money; he is a deadbeat and will never pay it back."
- "When I was child, my parents did not love me, and now I can't love anyone."
- "I am short and overweight; no one likes me. People reject me because of my appearance."
- "I lied to him but couldn't stop myself; it is beyond my control."

Can you find the facts in each of these? Look for what is indisputably true and not judgment or fantasy. Here are the stories once more, and the facts are in **bolded italics**.

- "Sure, ***I could ask Mary to go on a date***, but there is no use in asking; she won't go."
- "The way ***things are*** going, I am sure to lose my job and end up loosing everything."

- *"**There has been** a lot of **cancer in my family**, I know I will eventually get it and die."*
- *"**I** should have never **loaned my brother money**; he is a deadbeat and will never pay it back."*
- *"When **I was child**, my parents did not love me, and now I can't love anyone."*
- *"**I am short and overweight**; no one likes me. People reject me because of my appearance."*
- *"**I lied to him** but couldn't stop myself; it is beyond my control."*

The rest is all fear fiction. Maybe it is true, maybe it is not, so why believe the fear fiction? Fear fiction is scary and often *"predicts"* results and events as being far more damaging than they merit. Why would I do this to myself – make things appear worse than they are? I create fear fiction because I am programmed to do it. Ego keeps me in a state of protecting myself from being found out that I am not worthy of unconditional love, thus I am always on edge waiting for the inevitable. When a perceived threat appears, it is simply something that I already anticipated.

I create the worst-case scenario because I know that I am unworthy and deserve the worst. I do not know how much damage I will actually incur (if any) so I mentally prepare for disaster.

All this is based on nothing other than my imagination. The future is always unknown to me; I truly do not know for sure what will happen next. Fear fiction anticipates the worst. As a result of my story, beginning with the facts and then embellished with fear fiction, I opt to flee, to fight, or to flounder.

*Fear fiction is just that, false, yet it had me stuck in the rut of accepting the judgments of others **and myself** that I was unworthy.*

∞

Chapter 15 – Releasing fear fiction

If I am to break the cycle of fear that keeps me from loving myself, I must learn to release fear fiction. I must look at my story about what I fear and find the fear fiction. The way to do this is to examine every element of my story for judgment. Each judgment I find represents fear fiction.

For example, I pass a friend in the hallway. I say hello, and my friend ignores me, going on her way. I feel fearful. I am threatened that she now "sees" my unworthiness as being so extreme that I don't even merit a simple return greeting. She will probably tell others, gossip about me, ridicule me, and damage my reputation. What a hateful person she is!

Can you detect the fear fiction that I created? All that happened is I said hello and she did not. That's it. The rest is made up; it is my creation - fear fiction forecasting what will happen next. Is it true? Maybe, but it is highly unlikely. I simply don't know. How much time will I spend fretting and waiting for the inevitable assassination of my reputation that will probably never occur? It could be literally years.

What will my fear fiction do to my friendship with her? I will not trust her and will be on the alert for any nuance, hint, or any other signs that she "knows" I am not worthy.

Fear fiction destroys relationships, friendship, careers, and even lives. Is fear fiction worth allowing made-up expectations to rule my life to the point of despair?

I gain control of my life when I release fear fiction.

∞

Chapter 16 – Venting emotions

Venting emotion is my method for releasing fear fiction. Recognizing the emotion is necessary, but it is not sufficient to release fear fiction. Realizing that fear fiction creates anger or sadness is a necessary first step followed by venting.

To vent an emotion is to empty myself of the energy of the emotion. How? I relive the event to which the emotion is attached in as much detail as possible. Recalling the first time I experienced this emotion is ideal but not necessary. Recalling the most distant event in which I experienced the emotion is enough to begin release. Simply "seeing" the emotion in my memory's eye is not enough. The emotion must be "felt" in my heart's memory.

What was it like when this event occurred? Who was there? What happened? How did I feel? I re-experience those feelings even though they are painful, shameful, or frustrating. What do I want to do and say to those present in my memory? In my imagination I relive the event. I tell "them" how the event made me feel. I act out my emotions short of harming myself or anyone else. Scream, shout, cry, punch pillows, I let it all out. I must be physical in my venting; physical energy is necessary to a complete emptying.

This is the release. I keep at it until I am drained, until there is nothing left to release.

Safely venting my emotions releases both my fear fiction and my judgment on which the fear fiction was based.

∞

Chapter 17 – The gift of light

*As in the experience of all things, gratitude is appropriate.
When I release fear fiction through venting emotion, the
judgment associated with it is also gone. This opens me to the
possibility of sincerely expressing gratitude. For what am I
grateful, and how do I express my gratitude?*

I am grateful to no longer have the deep-rooted emotion that
gives rise to my judgment and fear. I have vented it and am
empty. I show my gratitude by filling the emptiness inside of
me where the emotion lay for so long without light. I do this
by asking for light to fill the void left by releasing the
unharmonious emotion. Judgment and unharmonious emotion
hide in the shadows of the past. They block the light. When I
vent them, the light can now flood in and illuminate the dark
corners of my past.

How does this work?

The ability to bring light into my energetic body to fill the
space vacated by the vented, heavy, unharmonious emotion is
enabled by the laws of energetics. Energetics tells me that my
energetic body (the combination of my physical, mental,
emotional bodies with my Soul and Higher Self) has a finite
capacity to hold energy. Energetics also specifies that my
energy must stay balanced, that is, when I release energy,
some form of energy must flow in to replace it. If I do not
consciously request a different form of energy than what I
released, then the same energy will be attracted to my
energetic body and fill the void.

If I vent unharmonious, heavy energy, and fail to ask for
another form of energy to replace it, I will, sooner or later,
receive more of the same. This phenomenon explains fights
that go and on. Each party to the fight releases angry, heavy,
energy only to receive the same energy in return released by
the "opponent" and cycling indefinitely, sometimes for years
or a lifetime. This continues until one person "wins" or both
retire, exhausted.

On the other hand, if, after I release angry, heavy energy, I ask for light to flow into the void created by the released angry energy, then I have no more angry energy to release. Regardless of what the other party does, the fight then ends. There is no longer any reason to fight, because by not reciprocating angry energy I have no reason for fighting. This is but one example. There are many, many others.

After the upheaval and stress that accompany emotional venting, I can go to that place within where unharmonious emotion once held sway, and which is now calm and be comforted in the presence of the light energy that now reposes there.

For this to work, I must have the awareness of my need for light. I must remember to ask for light, for if I do not, the nature of energy is such that, after I vent and release, my emptiness will attract more unharmonious emotion to refill itself. Bringing in light must be done with consciousness and gratitude.

I am grateful to God for the gift of light and my ability to fill my emptiness with it.

∞

Chapter 18 – The perfection of fact

My "story" about my fear consists of fear fiction and facts. When I release myself from the grip of fear fiction, what remains is fact. What do I do about the facts?

Subtracting fear fiction from my story around what I fear serves to remove fear, but what of the facts that remain? There is value in the surviving facts. First, however, I must ensure the facts <u>are</u> the facts. I do this by examining each fact. I pass a friend, and she does not return my greeting; that is what happened. These are the facts:

- I passed a friend.
- I greeted her.
- She did not return my greeting.

That is **all** that happened. I test each of the facts by asking myself if I have any judgment associated with the fact. If I do, there is still fear fiction remaining, and I need to discover and vent the underlying emotion. Judgment is simply legitimatized emotion. When all of the facts are without any emotion, I am able to accept them.

Acceptance is simply looking at the facts and being able to say that is what happened. It does not mean anything about anyone or me. It is simply what happened. There are many possible reasons as to why my friend did not return my greeting. I do not know which one is true, and it doesn't matter; it simply does not matter.

Fact is perfect. Anyway that I look at a fact, it is the same. When I know a fact, I am experiencing the perfection of life. If I cannot accept the fact, then I am creating karma and the future lessons it creates. When I accept the fact, I am experiencing unconditional love, and karma is released. Each fact is thus perfect, for it either teaches me love, or it sets up more opportunities to love.

There is one more aspect of acceptance to be considered, namely, I do not forgive people or myself. It may be a surprising statement, but consider this: Forgiveness is a judgment trap, because to forgive implies that someone is wrong. "Wrong" is a judgment and reflects my fear. If I simply lovingly accept what happened (the facts), then I am far more loving than if I "forgive." I realize that this flies in the face of what may be considered "spiritually correct," but I find acceptance works much better than forgiveness, for both the person I "accept" and for me.

My life is perfect.

∞

Chapter 19 – Reflexes and responses

It would be wonderful to say that once I release fear and judgment around an event in my past I am finished with them for good. Alas, it is not so. My spiritual body may be cleansed of the unharmonious emotion, but it remains in my mental body in the form of offensive and defensive strategies and tactics.

This is not a joyful condition. Strategies and tactics for protecting myself and earning conditional love are my mental creations. They are learned and thus are governed by the laws of learning. The laws of learning are powerful and inflexible:

- Most actions I take are responses to conditions that I encounter.
- I will continue to take these actions for as long as they appear to have value for me.
- The action-response phenomenon is called a reflex.
- A reflex occurs without benefit of awareness or thought.
- I cannot undo reflexes, but I can replace them with new ones.

New learning only occurs in the presence of awareness.

It is inevitable that my mental body/ego will initiate an old reflex, even though I have illuminated the darkness in my spiritual body. I will experience fear fiction. I will judge. What is different?

The difference lies in the illumination of my spiritual body accomplished through venting the emotion associated with the fear fiction. There is no longer the foundation for fear and judgment. I only need to have awareness to stop the fear-judgment chain reaction.

Pavlov's famous dogs continued to salivate when the dinner bell rang, even though food was absent. I begin to initiate the fear-judgment reflex, then my awareness kicks in and I realize that I do not have to "salivate." I can understand that the acceptance I experienced by quickly releasing the fear fiction is far more fulfilling than the unharmonious emotion that is the result of the fear-judgment reflex.

What does this take to bring about?

Practice, practice, practice, with attention on awareness, will bring about my new learning over time. In the interim, especially when I "fail" to have awareness until powerfully in the grip of fear, I accept my "shortcomings," and I do not abuse myself for not invoking awareness earlier. It took me years to develop these reflexes; they are not going to be replaced overnight.

My experience… As of the completion of this book in the year of 2003, I retain many of my fear-based reflexes. Perhaps one of the strongest is to want to defend myself when I am criticized. The reflex is to verbally attack the person who has "insulted" me, to lash out to divert the insulter from knowing for sure that I am unworthy. Often when the criticism is made, the emotions flash across the screen of my consciousness, and I want to reply in kind. Mostly now, the aware, awakened me heads off the tongue-lashing, and I can lovingly accept what was said, who said it, and myself. When I do this, harmony inevitably results.

I repeatedly release old fear-judgment based chain reactions until they are no longer reflexes.

∞

Chapter 20 - Awareness

*My awareness is the key to my spiritual evolution. Without
awareness, I stumble through life, unaware that the events and
people around me blow me about as a leaf before an ill wind.
I am reactive in the matter of how I lead my life. I have neither
harmony nor personal power.*

Awareness is not simple consciousness. Awareness is a higher
form of consciousness in which I discern that I have choices. I
am not bound to endlessly act in accordance with what I was
taught in the past. To do so is to live life as reactions and
reflexes. When I am reactive, I cannot break the patterns of
my past, and thus nothing changes in the quality of my life.

People, places, and things may change, but the results of my
interactions with them do not. I can only break these patterns
by becoming proactive. Becoming proactive demands
awareness. Awareness is simply knowing that I do not have to
react; awareness is asking myself the question, "What choices
do I have other than this reaction?"

Asking this question turns on the light of spiritual illumination.
Being aware finally gave me the control of my life that I
sought for so long. How did I learn to ask, "What choices do I
have other than this reaction?"

I learned to ask the question out of my disappointments and
perceived failures. When I discovered awareness I did not
immediately implement it before taking all actions. I remained
reactive. The powerful reflexes of the past did not easily yield
to new choices. I learned about a phenomenon that made
awareness possible in the moment before taking an action.

Even after I acted reflexively and reactively, if the
consequences of the action did not reflect love and
acceptance, then there was, as always, an unharmonious
emotion. Realizing the unharmonious emotion led me to
understand that I had choices other than the one I made. I had
"after the act awareness." Eventually the understanding that I

had choices led to having awareness of choices <u>before</u> taking action. That marked the beginning of having different results and improvement in the quality of my life.

My experience… as an ensign in the US Navy, my first duty station was a creaky old destroyer. I was in the operations department that had an officer in charge who delighted in terrorizing his junior officers. For over a year, I received vicious tongue lashings from him over the smallest infraction of hundreds of rules. For a long time, I simply quietly endured whatever he had to say and then slunk off with my tail between my legs. Then, one day I realized that I had a choice: I could take up for myself, so the next time he began an attack, I rallied and, in no uncertain terms, told him off for a change. The look on his face was priceless, and that was the end of my "suffering" at his hands.

I was not at all spiritually aware or awakened. I was only twenty-three at the time. Perhaps I would handle the situation differently now. The point is, although I did not think of it that way, I had the awareness of choice, and from that choice, created a difference in my life. It would be many years before I understood the implications of that day to spiritual evolution.

I choose my actions with awareness.

∞

Chapter 21 – Karma and the illusion of duality

The principles of duality and karma make it possible for me to understand the dynamics of spiritual living. Karma is simply the mechanism that teaches me to unconditionally love and accept everything, most of all, myself. The illusion of duality is the method whereby karma teaches. It is simple although it sometimes seems complex.

First, karma is <u>not</u> punitive negative "payment" for past misdeeds, or for being good or bad. Karma <u>is</u> opportunity. Since God's design for me is to learn to love myself, then providing a method for doing so is divine; hence, karma is divine. To learn to love myself unconditionally after primal abandonment when I discovered that love is conditional, I needed constant opportunities to practice loving. Karma provides exactly that.

Every action that I take, aware or not, is an opportunity to release karma or to intensify karma. I call them my "karmic moments." Intensifying karma simply places more pressure on me to learn unconditional love. Reducing karma occurs through my choice to unconditionally love whatever or whoever is present for me in the moment.

Any moment and situation can be a karmic moment. Here is how the mechanism works. Unhealed fears "attach" to certain kinds of events. When I encounter one of those events, for example being criticized by someone, the unhealed fear results in a judgment (I am unworthy), which then triggers an unharmonious emotion such as anger, hurt, disappointment, or frustration. At the point the unharmonious emotion surfaces, I have a choice: to <u>intensify karma</u> by <u>not loving</u> and accepting or <u>reducing karma</u> <u>by loving</u> and accepting.

An Event ➔ Unhealed fear ➔ Judgment ➔ Unharmonious emotion ➔ Choice

Karma exists within me. For me, there is no white-bearded accounting angel making debit and credit entries in a celestial register. My spiritual body is the "accountant," and there is only one account: how much do I unconditionally love and accept? The higher the balance in the account, the more easily I can exercise love in karmic moments. The lower the balance, the more fearful those <u>same</u> moments become.

This is the duality – the two-sided coin – a moment, any moment that can be either experienced with love or can be intensely feared. On one side of the duality coin is love (reducing karma) and on the other is fear (intensifying karma). The less I love, the more intense my fear becomes. Even when I am experiencing fear, my fear is really an illusion because love is <u>always</u> there; I only need to shift my awareness to access it. Love-fear duality is my greatest illusion.

The experience of fear and distress is not punishment. It is similar to studying a difficult subject (in my case mechanical drawing) in school that takes time to grasp when the subject is not obvious. Eventually I get it, the lesson is learned, and the fear of not being able to understand it goes away. There was no necessity to experience the fear and distress. I, not karma, create my own fear and distress by not exercising love and acceptance.

My karma is unrelenting and a divine gift.

∞

Chapter 22 – Intensifying and reducing karma

Intensifying and reducing karma are presented to me constantly. Every action I take is an opportunity to intensify my karma or to reduce it. I need not be aware of the mechanism; it will operate independent of my awareness. Awareness, however, is the only state of mind that eventually results in reducing my karma.

The first action that I took in my life when I acted out of fear opened my karmic account with a negative balance. For many years thereafter, the negative balance grew and grew. To be sure, there were loving actions that I took without being aware of their karma-reducing effect, but intensification outweighed reduction by a large proportion until something happened.

While I was a student at the University of Santa Monica, I developed a wonderful relationship with a fellow student. It was one of those rare encounters when you meet someone that you instantly "know." Not only was she a great friend, she was unrelenting in supporting me to heal. One night after class, we sat in her car talking, and something she said (neither she nor I remember specifically what it was) triggered me to plunge inside to the dark places within me.

For the next amount of time, I confronted all of the major primal abandonment events in my life. I cried, sobbed, screamed, and writhed around in my seat until finally I was spent, exhausted. I felt free for the first time in my memory. All of the heavy energy stored for so long in those dark places was gone. I was free of my past, and expressed my gratitude by lovingly accepting all of those events and the people who were in them.

The intensity of my accumulated karma finally caused me to cry out that night for the means to change my life. I heard myself and, thus, spirit opened my awareness to understanding the nature of karma: every action that I take is either done in love or fear. Since love and fear are a two-sided coin, I can turn any fear-side over and find love. Here's how.

What I do does not affect karma. **Why** I do what I do matters. Am I <u>reacting</u> to fear, attempting to "control" someone or something, and hiding my unworthiness? Or am I <u>proactively</u> applying unconditional love and acceptance, opening myself to whatever value there is in the karmic moment? It is the same event but with different states of mind.

This was not an easy principle for me to understand. When I think about taking a life, I wonder how that could be done lovingly. If I kill out of fear with the desire to eliminate my fear through the death of another person, then I intensify my karma. On the other hand, if the circumstances were such that taking the life (euthanasia, for example) was done with love and acceptance, then my karma is reduced.

God does not judge what I do. Humanity has created the concepts of good and evil, crime and punishment, and fear-based laws. This was unavoidable as a result of experiencing primal abandonment and the consequent feelings of separation from unconditional love. Once I decided that I was unworthy of unconditional love, then the strategies and tactics I developed were sometimes anti-social, and society responded with law, judgment, and punishment. This system is so ingrained in us, that we come to believe in good and evil, and thus we categorize actions as such. Nonetheless, understanding the difference between **what** I do and **why** I do it led me to the greater importance of why I act, versus the act itself.

I strive to maintain awareness of the "why" of my actions.

∞

Chapter 23 – Harmony in day-to-day life

Each of my days is composed of a series of moments in which I choose my state of being: love or fear. It is relatively simple to do this when I am aware in the moment. The challenge comes in linking moments of awareness together for sustained periods. When I accomplish this, harmony results. How do I know harmony?

I know harmony when I am loving. Loving is complete and unconditional acceptance of everyone and everything.

I know harmony when I am compassionate. Compassion is acknowledging that everyone is walking his or her path, and by not judging, I remove impediments from their paths.

I know harmony when I am humble. Humility is recognizing that God within us makes us all equal. I am no "better" or "worse" than anyone else.

I know harmony when I am in integrity. Integrity is speaking my truth from my heart without judgment.

I know harmony when I have courage. Courage is taking responsibility for my choices and actions, and their consequences.

Harmony is the goal of my moments and days.

∞

Chapter 24 – Mirror, mirror on the wall...

As much as I may try, I am not aware of harmony much of the time. What, then, can I use to bring me back to an awareness of harmony? Whenever I dislike, disapprove, or disdain, the object of my "dis" is reflecting some aspect of me. It is I looking into a mirror.

The aspect of me that I see in someone or something may be carefully hidden in my dark or shadow self. My ego protects it from the light, and it lurks ready to reveal itself only outside of me. How could I have such a distasteful quality!

I have them nonetheless. What I dislike that is outside of me is really something that I dislike about me, and yet, I am not conscious of it. In the perfect human system that God gave me, the dark and shadowy aspects of myself, although hidden by ego, are revealed in what I do not like. It is in my dislike and disapproval that the fears I hold become conscious. Moving consciousness to awareness provides the opportunity to release fear.

At last I know where to begin my healing process. It is by looking into the mirror of experience. Whatever disfigured, fun house image I see is really I, as I secretly perceive myself.

*My experience...*If I saw someone driving dangerously or carelessly, I would become angry and at the least, mutter under my breath about what a jerk he was to endanger me. At the worst, I might chase after him on the highway and salute him with an obscene gesture, which can get interesting. I know now that these drivers were mirroring back to me my own behaviors that I did not want to recognize in myself. Once I understood that, I shifted my attitude about other drivers to one of compassion... well, at least most of the time.

The mirror others hold in front of me reveals what I have left to heal.

∞

Chapter 25 – Healing process

*Healing the wounds of primal abandonment, the fear that I
cannot be loved for who I am, is my primary focus, for I know
that without doing so I will not experience the fulfillment and
harmony that come with fully loving myself. I learned a
"process," a method for healing. I also learned that only I can
heal myself. Alas, no one could do it for me.*

A process is any procedure or method that is performed over
and over. It can be refined along the way; however, its
purpose remains to ultimately achieve the same outcome. My
healing process is threaded throughout *A Tao of God*. The
goal here is to simply summarize my process in one place so it
can easily be read from beginning to end. I must emphasize
that it is **my** healing process, and I willingly share it with the
caveat that your discernment is needed to determine its
applicability to you. What you can use, I gladly give.

> 1. My **starting point** occurs whenever I am **aware**
> that I am **judging** how life should be other than what
> it is. (Chapters 11-13)
> 2. I **create** a "story" around what I would have to be
> different. I describe what happened (or is happening)
> by putting into words the beginning, middle, and end
> of the event. I then determine the point (or theme) of
> the story as succinctly as I can. (Chapter 14)
> 3. I **break down the story** into fear fiction (what I
> made up that is not necessarily true) and the facts, the
> elements of the story that actually happened. (Chapter
> 15)
> 4. I **release** fear fiction by venting the unharmonious
> emotions I have attached to what I made up. I recall
> and relive my earliest recollection of the
> unharmonious emotion. I vent the resulting emotions
> until they are spent. (Chapter 16)
> 5. I give **gratitude** for the healing of this "dark place"
> by filling the dark where the emotion hid with light,
> thereby denying the released emotional energy from
> attaching itself to me again. (Chapter 17)

6. I **accept** the facts as being perfect. Acceptance is simply looking at the facts and being able to say, that is what happened. It does not mean anything about anyone or me. (Chapter 18)

7. A **reflex** remains that will call forth the memory of the unharmonious emotion in certain situations. I learn a new reflex using the relevant steps of my process. (Chapter 19)

8. **Awareness** is essential to invoking my process and to quickly recognizing future occurrences of the emotion. (Chapter 20)

9. **Karma** is reduced each time I successfully work my healing process. (Chapter 21)

No one can heal me except me, and my process is the means by which I become healed.

∞

Manifesting Passion

Chapter 26 - Intention

Once I began to heal and truly learn to love myself, one of the greatest challenges to being human confronted me: how to have the abundance that I needed to live as an aware, spiritually-evolving person?

Intention is the first step in manifesting abundance. Abundance is having just a bit more than I need. Having abundance allows me to set aside concerns of not being able to live in my passion because of real lack, not the fears associated with never having enough to feel secure (which is a fantasy).

Humans are powerful manifestors and creators – far more than most of us imagine. Giving intent is my instruction to myself or the Universe about what I need. It is a formal declaration, and as such, has form. The form is useful, a type of checklist, enabling me to ensure that I include all of the information specifying what I need to manifest and why.

Intention is about specifying what I want and why I want it. Spirit, the Universe, or God works on the who, when, where, and how of the intention. Many elements must come together to deliver what I need, and I have no direct means of bringing them together, so I need support.

The "when" of my intention is very important to understand. The more complex my intention, the more elements must be brought into play for the intention to manifest, and the longer it may take to bring the elements together. I can only give intent for myself because of the gifts of free will and choice; therefore, my intentions cannot be imposed on others. My intention can only be manifested when it is in the highest and best interests of all concerned.

Intention is the mechanism whereby I manifest my needs.

∞

Chapter 27 – Personal and Universal

There are two types of intention: personal and Universal. They are differentiated by how manifestation is accomplished: either within my energetic body or by the Universe. The form of my intention is different for each one.

"I direct manifesting (**my personal** need) in my highest and best interest." A personal need is one in which I have the necessary resources within my energetic body to manifest. For example, if I have a headache, I can give intent for my physical body to heal my headache: "I direct manifesting the healing of my headache in my highest and best interest."

There is no intervention required from the Universe because my body can heal the headache. Notice the use of the word "direct" instead of "intent." I am, in effect, ordering my energetic body to deliver on the need I stated in a manner that is in my highest and best interest. I can do this because I am dealing solely with myself.

"I give intent to manifest (**my Universal** need) in my highest and best interest." A Universal need is one I cannot accomplish on my own, for example, finding a publisher for a book I wrote. Manifesting a Universal need requires cooperation from the Universe outside of me. I cannot manifest for another person, so for me to say, "I give intent to manifest Random House publishing my book in my highest and best interest," is to specify that people within Random House must publish my book. The Universe will not act on my behalf when I dictate to people.

The more complex my Universal intention, the longer it may take to manifest because the Universe has to line up all of the conditions I specify. The Universe may also adjust my intention to actually manifest what is in my highest and best interest, and that may not be what I think it should be.

Last, any intention (or direction) should be free of fear. If my intention is based in fear, then I will receive the opportunity to experience more fear in return, rather than what I thought I was requesting. For my intentions to work, they must be based in love and acceptance, not fear. Awareness is a powerful tool for "bench checking" my intention before releasing it.

I can only manifest for myself that which is in my highest and best interest.

∞

Chapter 28 - Cooperation

In my three dimensional human world, cooperation is necessary to get things done in my day-to-day existence. The examples of cooperation are endless; our society depends on them. Few of us could survive if it were not for cooperation at many levels for even the most insignificant of actions. If I buy a loaf of bread in a market, hundreds of people from bakers to assembly line workers, to office management and administration, to drivers, to distributors, to more drivers, market operators, market employees, and so on, must cooperate to get that loaf of bread on the shelf. And that is only scratching the surface…

I may not think about the production, distribution, and retail supply chain making it possible to buy the loaf of bread, but I would never presume the loaf of bread shows up simply because I thought of it. However, at one time I thought of manifesting via intention to be both automatic and somehow magic, and was disappointed over and over. Why?

I was not recognizing that cooperation is needed in the Universe to manifest my intentions. The good news is I do not have to understand or explain the "supply chain" that causes my intention to manifest. That is the Universe's job, and it is far better equipped to figure out the who, where, when, and how than I am.

The other news is that there are some requirements I must satisfy in order to clearly request cooperation. They are passion, gratitude, and self-worth.

When I recognize the need for Universal cooperation in manifestation, I engage the interconnectedness of everything.

∞

Chapter 29 - Passion

Passion is the driving force behind my intention. The degree of my passion determines the amount of energy I flow into my intention. Energetics teaches that energy seeks equilibrium, and the amount of energy flowing "out" will be balanced by the amount of energy flowing "in." Consequently, the passion I have for my intention influences the quality of cooperation with the Universe. What, then, is passion?

Passion, with respect to intention, is determined by the degree that my intention is in my highest and best interest. My highest and best interest reflects the expression of who I am as a spiritual being, not a human being. It speaks, not only to loving myself; it speaks also to who I am with respect to others. Passion is not about me; it is about others.

How do I know passion? I know that I am in my passion when what I do flows effortlessly and leaves me harmonious and fulfilled. Often, passion is associated with human-based accomplishments that leave me spent and dissatisfied. That is not passion; instead it is the release of emotional energy in the hope that the release will bring harmony and fulfillment, but it does not.

How do I express passion in my intention? After I state my intention, I describe the passion that I have for my intention's manifestation. After I state, "I give intent to manifest publishing my book in my highest and best interest," I add my passion description, "In publishing my book, the knowledge it contains will support others in finding their own paths."

My passion is the "why" of my intention.

∞

Chapter 30 – Gratitude

The next step in preparing my intention after its statement and passion description is to give gratitude. The gratitude that is appropriate is an expression of how I will feel when my intention is manifested. Is it not appropriate to express gratefulness for the satisfaction of my passion?

To be effective, gratitude needs to be heartfelt. If I am passionate about manifesting my intention, then I should be grateful for its ultimate manifestation.

Adding to the declaration of my intention, "I give intent to manifest the publication of my book in my highest and best interest. In publishing my book, the knowledge it contains will support others in finding their own paths (my passion statement)…" I then add my expression of gratitude, "…for which I am grateful because of the benefit to the Earth when its readers are then moved to seek their own spiritual awakenings."

Expressing gratitude for the manifestation of my intention adds further energy to it.

∞

Chapter 31 – Self-worth

The last component of the intention declaration is self-acknowledgment to the Universe that I am worthy of having my intention manifested. This step is actually a last check to ensure there is no fear contained within the "why" of my intention. Having even a tinge of fear hidden in the "why" of my intention will cause the intention to fail to manifest in the manner I requested.

The destructive role of fear in declaring an intention must be understood in order for me to manifest what I need. The laws of intention are such that what is manifested is the lowest level of energy (usually fear) contained within the intention. Usually, I am not conscious that fear lurks unnoticed within the energy of my intention. For example, if I declare an intention to have a lot of money, and my "why" for the money is an unconscious fear of being homeless for lack of money, what gets manifested is more fear, probably around money.

Fear energy is at a lower vibration than love and light energy, so the higher aspect of my intention is not manifested. The lack of understanding about this aspect of intention explains why so many of my past intentions seemingly never manifested. What I now know is that they did manifest in the form of karmic moments so I could once again have the opportunity to experience love and reduce my karma.

The complete declaration of my intention looks like this:

In the name of spirit:

I give intent to manifest publishing my book in my highest and best interest. *(Intention statement)*
In publishing my book, the knowledge it contains will support others in finding their own paths... *(Passion)*
... for which I am grateful because of the benefit to the Earth when its readers are moved to seek their spiritual awakenings. *(Gratitude)*
I am unconditionally worthy to have this intention manifested. *(Self-worth)*

So it is.

This format is long, so to ensure I stay on track, I write it down, and when ready to send it to the Universe, I add, **In the name of spirit...** before the intention statement. The last sentence, **So it is,** "seals" the envelope and drops it in the cosmic mailbox.

After using this format for a while, I discovered I could drop the passion, gratitude, and self-worth formal wording because they became automatic thoughts in my intention process. Remember, my process is just that – mine – and your discernment will lead you to your own.

I am a very powerful manifestor and creator using my power with awareness, carefully and wisely, to manifest what I need.

∞

Chapter 32 – Attention

Attention is the twin of intention. Intention sets forth the request for manifestation. Attention helps to further energize the intention and move it along.

It is very difficult (probably impossible) for me to have consciousness of more than one thought at a time. In the moment-by-moment nature of human existence, I am choosing thoughts, or they are popping unbidden into my mind. Awareness and choosing my thoughts are instrumental in helping to energize my intention. The more energy I put into my intention, the easier it is for the Universe to manifest.

The moments when I am aware of my intention add energy to the intention. Think of it as anticipation. For example, let's assume that I am hungry and anticipate sitting down soon to my favorite meal. I think about the food, its smell, taste, and appearance. Just like one of Pavlov's conditioned dogs, I may even salivate. All of the attention that I place on my forthcoming meal adds energy to the manifestation of the food.

Attention is a further reflection of the passion associated with my intention. The more strongly and deeply I need my intention to manifest, the more attention I place on its manifestation. It is as simple as thinking about my intention manifested, just like anticipating eating a fine meal. It is being inside the experience of the manifestation. This is the essence of attention – having the awareness of my intention as the Universe is in motion to manifest it.

It is important not to let fear creep into attention. The purity of love (unconditional self-worth) in my intention needs to be maintained in attention. When anticipating, it is easy for me to have a tendency to think that my intention will not be manifested. To prevent changing the "work order" of my intention to embody fear, I need to keep checking my sense of worthiness to have my intention manifested.

I attend to that which I intend.

∞

Chapter 33 – Action

"… action," Oscar Wilde wrote, *"is a mode of purification."* It also accelerates manifesting my intention. Attention to my intention adds energy to the intention; action adds energy exponentially. The more energy I put into my intention being manifested, the easier it is for the Universe to provide. It is said that the <u>one</u> <u>common</u> <u>characteristic</u> of all successful people is <u>not</u> intelligence, knowledge, beauty, wealth, position, or physical ability; it is <u>persistence</u>.

There is a saying within the Judeo-Christian tradition to the effect that, "God helps those who help themselves." This saying is a reflection of the importance of action. When I need something enough to give intent to manifest it, I am prepared to be in action to assist in its manifestation.

The introductory quote of Oscar Wilde's is very relevant to me. Being in action about anything is cleansing. Instead of fretting or wondering about an intention, doing something about it always lifts me. When I act on my intentions there is a double benefit. First, I energize my intention, and second, there is the satisfaction of being a part of the manifestation.

I know I am a powerful manifestor, as indeed we all are. For most of my life, I didn't know how to powerfully manifest, and now I do. Since we are all God, we share in God's ability to manifest. My humanness places some limitations on me; nonetheless, I have the ability to manifest what I need in my human experience. This only makes sense. Why would God allow me to be here to accomplish a task and not give me the necessary tools?

The intention process, along with attention and <u>action</u>, is a very powerful aid to manifesting. Howsoever you word your intentions is a personal thing and a product of your own intuition and discernment. Each of us can have our own personal and unique way of declaring intentions. The important point is to have <u>some</u> method of doing so.

What then is being in action all about?

Being in action is not necessarily doing the "right" thing; it is being "right" in what I do. "Right" here is in the sense of how directly does my action contribute to manifesting my intention? If I plant an apple tree, working salt into the soil around the new tree does not contribute to the tree's growth. However, I could water the tree, prune it, fertilize it, talk to it, play music for it, and so on. All of these possible actions contribute to the tree's growth; some are more effective than others. The degree of effectiveness is not crucial.

What is crucial is that I am frequently in action on behalf of my intention. I do not attempt to calculate or determine what the "best" action is. I have no way of ever definitely knowing the best action, not even in retrospect. A good practice is to read my intention declaration often, especially in the days following its release to the Universe. Any action that supports manifesting my intention works. I am not concerned that my action is the best one. I don't even know what that is!

I choose being in action about my intention, rather than inaction.

∞

Chapter 34 – Patience... and faith

Universal intentions require the cooperation of the Universe to manifest. I cannot know what diverse elements need to be brought together in what sequence to create my request. I also do not know the exact form of the manifestation; sometimes it is much more subtle than expected, and I need to be alert, less it passes by unnoticed.

After releasing an intention, I also accept that I must be patient and wait for what comes. The wait may be very short, or it may be a long time: months or years. The manifestation of my intention may not be what I thought I asked for. Remember, when asking for what is in my highest and best good, I leave the interpretation of what that is to the Universe.

Belief and faith play roles as well. Do I believe that my intention will manifest, or do I have faith that it will? There is a big difference. Belief is thinking that my intention will *probably* manifest. Faith is the certainty that my intention will manifest. What separates the two: belief and faith?

When I *commit* to the *certainty* of the manifestation of my intention, I have faith. This is not expectation; expectation seeks to dictate what will happen; faith is certainty that *something* will happen, and it may take many guises, depending on what is in my best and highest interest.

For example, I had faith that this book would be published. I did not know how or when. I knew that it would, and it was. In fact it was published in a way that I did not anticipate when I voiced my intention around it. I was willing to let the "way" it was published to come forth as I was in action to get it published. All of the elements of manifestation come together if I allow them.

Impatience can lead to believing that the intention is not going to manifest. So guess what? Since I believe it's not "going to happen," I unconsciously communicate that to the Universe, and the Universe responds by canceling the intention. After all, that's what I ordered, so that's what I got. I am reminded to be careful what I wish for…

Manifestations come when they are ready to come. Attention and action help to move them forward but cannot be used to guarantee a delivery date. In fact, placing a delivery date in an intention statement will be considered, but there are no guarantees. The "highest and best good" phrase can void a requested date because it may not be possible to manifest my intention at that time.

Consider that I want to buy a specific house. Someone is living in the house at present, and the house is not for sale. I present an intention to buy the house within 60 days. That can only happen if the present owner <u>chooses</u> to sell. The Universe will not compel the present owner to put the house up for sale simply to satisfy my intention. Manifesting all Universal intentions involves cooperation and win-win results.

Manifesting does not require someone to lose in order for someone else to gain, nor can it involve overriding someone's freedom to choose. This is in opposition to the principle of balance. Win-lose is a human invention – there is a Universe full of energy for all of us to share. We cannot co-create for others; to do so would be to deny them their exercise of free will.

My patience is not only a virtue; it is a necessity for my manifestations.

∞

Chapter 35 – No attachment

When I have an attachment to the outcome of my intention, I set myself up for failure and disappointment. I specify the what and the why of my intention, and the Universe attends to the where, how, when, and who. If I specify any of the Universe's tasks, I am attached to the outcome. I am changing the "work order" of my intention, and the Universe responds accordingly.

If I direct my intention be manifested by 10 AM next Friday, and the Universe is not aligned to deliver at that specific time, then when the "deadline" comes and passes without my intention manifesting, I am likely to think, "Well, there's another one that didn't work," and guess what? I just sent an order based in fear that cancels the original intention.

The Universe moves in mysterious ways; at least it seems that way, because I cannot know all of the actions that must happen in order to manifest my intention. If I could manifest the object of my intention, then I would simply do it. If I need a drink of water, I go get a drink of water. If I need a new job and can't find it, then I state an intention.

Fear, impatience, and expectation are major reasons for intention failure. These reasons are tricky because they can occur <u>after</u> I make my intention declaration. How I practice attention and action can help me stay focused on keeping my intention "alive" and ongoing. At a minimum, I need to keep fear from creeping into my intention and to have patience.

What if I become fearful, expectant, or impatient? Have I cancelled my intention?

Maybe, maybe not. Just as few Universal intentions are manifested immediately, cancellation due to fear, expectation, or impatience does not happen immediately. It is difficult, if not impossible, to prevent thoughts from popping into our minds, and some of those thoughts may be centered on fear, expectation, or impatience. If I take action to consciously release those thoughts, then my intention stays intact. It is only when I dwell on these thoughts and surrender to them that my intention is likely to be cancelled.

What I expect, I usually don't get.

∞

Living Life

Chapter 36 – Daily living

I tried evolving spiritually by performing rituals (meditation), and participating in planned events (seminars, satsangs, meetings), and although informative and inspiring, my life did not transform as a result. I became confused and disappointed when my daily existence did not deliver what I needed: harmony and fulfillment. It was not until I focused on how I lived my life moment by moment that I realized what I needed to do to have life be different.

Awareness in the moment is the key to all spiritual evolution. In each moment I have a choice as to how I will be: loving or fearful. Loving is natural; fearful is man-made. Is it possible to be loving in every moment of every day? I know that, for me, it is not. I think this is true of most, if not all, people.

The more moments that I spend as a loving and accepting human, the greater is my evolution as a spiritual being. What do I do in those loving moments? Here is a list of suggestions based on my experience:

- The simplest is to look around and within myself, and unconditionally accept whatever and whoever is present.
- If I cannot accept whatever and whoever is present, then I use my healing process on the spot to shift into acceptance.
- Attend to my intentions.
- Express gratitude to the Universe for who I am and what I have.
- Think of actions I can take to help manifest my intention.
- Ground and center myself through breathing.
- Perform an unselfish act.

It is possible to <u>be</u> loving acceptance in any moment regardless of what action I am doing, even working, driving, and so on. With practice, loving acceptance becomes a "background program" that operates concurrently with whatever I am "doing." Being fearful is not natural. Loving is. I have been trained to be fearful, but my loving essence is always present if I allow it to come forth into my consciousness.

Being loving in the moment takes practice. I am not conditioned by my society to spend much time loving, so I work to recondition myself. All I really need is awareness; the rest is easy once my awareness is present. Without it, I will continue automatically reacting and responding as I have been trained to do since infancy.

When I realize that I have not been loving, I do not lament the fact or beat up myself. I take the realization as an opportunity to accept, that for awhile, I was not loving. After all, there is always the next moment, and the next, and the next. The past is past, and I cannot change it.

I am loving in as many moments as I can.

∞

Chapter 37 – Measuring progress

As I walk my path with the awareness of what is needed to evolve spiritually, I need to measure my progress. I think this is from my human "score card" mentality, and it also helps me to look at areas of my life that are still containing fear. It would be great to measure the moments of the day when I am loving and accepting. However, to do so is not practical, so the measurement I use is the quality and quantity of my relationships.

For me, a relationship is built around the exchange of needs. I call that WYGIN-WIGYN (wiggin-wiggin) or What You Got I Need and What I Got You Need. Without the exchange of "needs," there is no relationship. In every relationship, each person plays a role that affects how the relationship operates. The roles are defined in terms of strategies formed as a result of primal abandonment. There are always only two people in one relationship, and there are four roles or strategies that either person can play:

- **Dominants** attempt to control the other person and thereby prevent him or her from discovering the dominator's "unworthiness."
- **Submissives** surrender control in an effort to be whatever the other person wants him or her to be and in doing so, avoid having his or her "unworthiness" revealed.
- **Avoiders** are often passive-aggressive personalities who pretend to accept domination (or submission), but use subterfuge to avoid being found out as "unworthy." They will momentarily do or say what they perceive will get the other person to back off. Avoiders then revert to sabotage or lying to protect their unworthiness from discovery.

The three roles described above occur when each person in the relationship seeks to hide or divert attention from his or her unworthiness. It takes a lot of energy and time to do this.

What would happen if neither person was driven to play one those roles?

- **Partners** are not concerned with being judged unworthy since they have learned to *lovingly accept* themselves, and thus, the other person in the partnership; this is the most spiritual form of relationship.

The partner role is based on unconditional acceptance, open communication, and honesty. I seek to have as many of my relationships be partnerships as possible. If I am in a relationship that is other than partner-partner, then the relationship is a mirror that reflects some fear-based aspect of me that has not healed.

Partner-partner relationships can be subtle. For example, a seeming dominant-submissive relationship on the surface can actually be a partner-partner relationship if the two roles are what each person respectively needs at that point in his or her life. If both people are truly lovingly accepting of the other, then there is a partner-partner relationship. Sometimes it is easy to judge a relationship as being unsuccessful when viewed from by someone outside the relationship.

All that really matters in a partnership is dual, loving acceptance. The trappings that the relationship takes on can be deceiving. The difference is loving acceptance. If one or both people are trying to control each other, then there is an absence of dual, loving acceptance, and one of the other three roles accurately fits.

Measuring my spiritual progress is a matter of categorizing my relationships and using the ones with combinations of dominant, submissive, and avoidance roles to determine what I need to heal. I can measure my progress anytime I wish, and I can take appropriate action (use my healing process) whenever I choose. The more frequently I make the measurement and take appropriate action, the faster I evolve.

My healing process also works well in the moment when I am aware of the roles played by me and another person. If our relationship is anything other than partner-partner, I can immediately look at the mirror image of who I am and choose to use my healing process then and there.

Relationships are necessary to my survival, and partner-partner relationships make survival (and life) harmonious and fulfilling.

∞

Chapter 38 – Supporting others

The way I see it, there are three jobs associated with spiritual evolution. Job one is learning self-love. Job two is manifesting what I need to live my passions. Job three is supporting others in accomplishing jobs one and two. After all, I am connected to everything in the Universe, and thereby, to all of my fellow humans. Moreover, the more people who are aware of how to evolve and take action to do so, the better life is for all of us.

I know that I am a teacher, and I believe that all of us are teachers. We don't have to be teaching formally in classrooms to serve as teachers. I define teaching as presenting information. We present information to others all the time. Much of it is not factual, but rather, consists of judgments, opinions, rumors, gossip, stories, fear fiction, and so on. All information has the potential to influence, so whatever springs from my mouth and fingers has the power to influence.

As I evolved, I discovered that I could support others in their evolution. I do so, much in the way that *A Tao of God* is written, not as a "how to... this is what you must do" manual, but through sharing what I experienced and accepted as personal truth. My most effective teaching comes from exercising *personal power*. The three components of personal power are:

- When I speak, I speak my truth, and whether or not to speak is always a choice.
- I do what I say I am going to do. If I don't, I clean it up as fast as possible.
- I use discernment about what I hear and read before passing it on to others.

To do this requires awareness. Anytime that I am with others, or in the act of preparing information to be read or heard by others, I am in a virtual classroom. Awareness helps to prevent me from "teaching" judgment and other unharmonious emotional-based concepts as "facts." Doing so accomplishes two things. First, the <u>content</u> of what I communicate may be of value to someone's evolution. Second, the <u>context</u> of communicating from my personal power may cause others to see the possibility of doing the same.

The most powerful support of others is a combination of content and context. When the two of these come together as truth from the heart, the teaching that occurs is extremely effective. No one needs to be trained or certified to do this. All of us already possess the necessary tools to teach powerfully and compassionately with dashes of humor and humility thrown in. The most influential teaching is always one-on-one.

I support others in evolving by "teaching" from a position of personal power, and I am always teaching.

∞

Chapter 39 – The end game

The end game of spiritual evolution has no end. My experience leads me to believe that I will continue learning and evolving until I die. As a human, I will never be finished with evolving myself. I continue to intensify and reduce karma. I experience moments when I am in the state of fear. I judge. At times I give up my personal power. At times I am not loving and accepting. At times I am not patient. At times I do not have faith. At times I allow fear to enter my intention. At times I attach expectations to my intention. At times I do not support others in their evolution by teaching fear. At times I doubt my divinity. All of the time, I am a human being.

The real message of this chapter is not a litany of my shortcomings as an evolving human; the message is that, although I am perfect, I experience times when my perfection seems to have taken a holiday. When this happens, I do not take myself seriously or feel that I have disappointed God. God is indifferent to the judgments I make about myself and others. I believe God set us up to exist in harmony, and if we do not, that is all right, too. God does not judge, punish, criticize, or experience disappointment. God is the Universal spectator (or voyeur) and created our game of life so God could experience Itself.

That's it folks. There isn't anything else. The rest I made up, and so did you!

I am perfect and so are you. Why am I perfect? I am perfect because I reflect God, who is perfect. I am perfect because each moment of my life is an opportunity to reduce karma through unconditional acceptance and love, or to be reminded that I can be unconditionally accepting and loving, or to intensify karma – my choice. Reducing karma makes life easier because I need fewer and fewer "karmic moments" to remind me to practice acceptance and love, and so fewer "difficult" situations are placed in my path. What a perfect system! I am either rewarded for practicing loving acceptance, or I am presented with opportunities in which I can choose loving acceptance. Blessed if I don't, and blessed if I do.

The object of the game of life is for me to love myself, truly and thoroughly. When I do not love myself, karma keeps putting my non-love in my face. It took me a long time (over 50 years) to learn that simple formula. Now it seems so odd that I did not learn it earlier. I am grateful I finally did. I transformed my life, and in so doing I found the harmony and fulfillment that had eluded me for so long.

My end game as a human is really an unending game, and what fun it is.

∞

Concluding thoughts...

After finishing the preceding 39 chapters of *A Tao of God,* I concluded that a summary of what I learned could be helpful - a condensation of the results of walking my path as nine "findings."

1. Question everything.
Belief is a form of slavery with bonds that are forged for decades. Our belief chains are old and strong, sometimes wrapping around lifetimes. Their construction starts early in life when the powers of discernment and intuition are easily defeated by the perceived wisdom of those who are older and in control. By the time we have enough experience to question our beliefs, they are so ingrained that, for the most part, we do not question them.

By questioning everything, we begin to create personal truths that carry us forward on a personal path of evolution. The difference between a personal truth and a belief is that a personal truth is your creation, not something handed down to you, perhaps for generations. A personal truth is the product of your experience tempered in the fire of intuition and pounded into shape on the forge of discernment. It "fits." It feels "right." It raises no questions in your thoughts about its validity. In the here and now of its creation, it is the truth. Tomorrow may hold a different outcome, for experience in the form of karma continuously shapes our lives.

By questioning everything, we tend our garden of beliefs, weeding out the ones that do not serve our best and highest good, replanting those that serve as personal truths, and leaving a lot of vacant soil for later use. By questioning everything we begin to drill down into the core of our very being and discover who we truly are.

2. We are not alone.
Belief systems, dogma, law, custom, and habit have alienated us from one another and Spirit. I speak of the realization that the Earth is a huge ecosystem of everything that exists on it,

animate, inanimate, biological, and physical. Humans, as much as some of us pretend otherwise, <u>are</u> part of this system. The system, in fact, exists to support us. Sir Isaac Newton said of the universal reach of gravity, "Touch a flower and trouble a star." I can think of no better metaphor to illustrate how we each affect one another and the planet through our actions, as small as they may seem. Why, then, do we not embrace our interconnectedness?

Fear is the active ingredient that keeps alienation in place. Whenever we can release fear, even for a few moments, we can sense, explore, and appreciate our connectedness with all things. We then experience the love and beauty of Spirit. I had no idea that Spirit waited patiently for me to communicate. From my first energy rush I knew I was not alone. My life has not been the same since. Imagine moving from a position of feeling separate from the Earth and acknowledging nothing that could not be scientifically proven, to the realization that there was more to me, and to the world than I had believed and that there was something to this Spirit stuff. I knew because finally, I felt it.

3. "Fear is the mind killer."
I first read this expression in Frank Herbert's epic science fiction novel, *Dune*. Fear dominates the lives of most of us. We live out our days in fear, and it does kill the mind. Experiencing love of self and God is impossible while we are in the grip of fear. When fear is present, nothing else can be present. But overcoming fear is not the answer. Clenching one's teeth and plowing through a fearful state does not eliminate or release fear.

We fear God, each other, the planet, unseen and unknown "forces," and, most of all, we fear ourselves. In fact, all fear begins with our learning to fear ourselves. Fear of ourselves begins with primal abandonment, which is defined in Chapter 8 as the moment when, at some level of knowing, we experience the absence of love. From that moment on we live in a state of quiet terror that the absence of love is imminent. We behave in all manner of ways to create relationships that we hope will prevent the withdrawal of love. In fact, the manner in which we create and sustain our relationships with all things measures who we are at any moment.

4. Love is always available to us.

How paradoxical our lives are! On one hand, we strive so diligently to do those things that we believe will "earn" us the love of our partners, children, parents, bosses, teachers, friends, pets, and so on, while on the other hand, love is abundantly and simply available. We need but open to and accept it. It is even free. After all of the money we spend, hopefully seeking and maintaining love, the real thing is right in front of us – everywhere we go and in everything we do.

No matter how desperate the situation appears, no matter how dark the tragedy, or how unjust the crime, love is present in everything. Love is Universally present. In fact, there is nothing *but* love. Accessing love thus becomes the task, should we choose to take it on.

There is a concept introduced in Chapter 5, "Contrast creates distinction." We cannot know the existence of something until that something is absent. A fish has no distinction of water until it is taken from the water. The existence of "not water" becomes shockingly and quickly evident to the fish. When primal abandonment inevitably occurs, we learn the distinction "not-love" through the sudden absence of love, just like the fish pulled from its familiar environment of water learns that there is "not-water." How, then, do we access love in and out of the water of human existence? The next findings deal with that question.

5. Everything is perfect.

We are preconditioned to experience primal abandonment, and thus we seek to regain love through karma. When we do not practice love, we increase karma. Karma is not punishment, nor is it "debt." Karma is simply that which, in human form, we have yet to learn, namely, that everything is perfect, that everything is love. The only existence of "not love" is in our minds, thus, fear (the absence of love) is indeed the mind killer. Karma is a form of energy that we carry with us, which attracts events and situations that provide us with the opportunity to choose love rather than fear. This requires awareness.

Karma is the mechanism for the opportunity to focus awareness on the existence of love in any situation or relationship. When we realize in the moment, howsoever terrible or wonderful it may be, that there is nothing but love, we reduce the energy of karma. If we do not focus, accept, and, thereby, reduce karma in that moment, there will be many opportunities to do so in the future. Everything is perfect, because we are either in a state of love or in a state reminding us to love. As humans, we only exist in either the state of increasing karma or reducing karma. Karma is the blessing of Spirit, leading us to the love of Self and then to love of the Universal Self that is everything, the One, God.

6. Awareness is the gateway to love.
Without awareness, we doom ourselves to walk the days of lives, as I did for so many decades, feeling alone, fearful, and without hope. This kind of existence is an illusion. It is karma at work, not punishing us, but giving us greater and greater opportunities to love. The greater the injustice, the more horrible the event, the more fearsome the threat, the stronger the frustration, the greater is the opportunity to reduce karma through love and acceptance. All fear is an illusion. If I am plunging towards the Earth in an airplane, or find myself pinned down by a hungry tiger, the personal truth of the situation is that I am probably going to die shortly. So?

If I believe I am not alone and never have been alone, then death is simply the closing of one chapter and the opening of another. If I can, in the moment of death, achieve perfect clarity of awareness and accept that there is love present even then, I reduce karma and find love in the last fragment of human thought before the mind and body cease functioning, and Spirit is once more released to fully embrace Divinity. Everything is perfect.

7. Ego is the servant of fear.

There are many definitions of ego. The one I am about to give you is unique, insofar as I know: "Ego is the total collection of strategies and tactics that a human creates in order to acquire love, or to avoid losing love, in the certainty that love exists outside of him or herself." Ego holds the monster of fear at bay for a while, now and then, and is enough benefit for us to continue to nourish it. Ego creates judgment, opinion, and assumption. Ego cements belief into "truth." Ego becomes the pattern for living. Remember my life's mantra of, *"Don't screw up, make waves, or get caught?"* We all create a mantra and then hone it to a perfect edge, which we use to cut our way through life.

Unraveling the ego (accessing love) is entirely possible. The first step is to have awareness that you are in a state of ego (fear) by understanding that you are, in the moment, experiencing judgment, opinion, assumption, or perhaps un-camouflaged fear. Without this awareness, there is no opportunity at that time to access love. The second step is simply to accept whatever is present around which you have judgment, opinion, assumption, or obvious fear, <u>for whatever is confronting you is perfect</u>. It is the messenger of karma. Accept the situation for what it is, an opportunity to reduce karma and to have love fill the vacuum.

Another way of expressing this simple (but not necessarily easy) concept was taught to me at the University of Santa Monica: "It's not the issue; it's how we relate to the issue." This one statement is profound in its implications for releasing karma and accessing love. I have heard many people speak of some event that they deem negative, as being a direct reflection of karma. For example, a driver may hit the fender of an unoccupied car in a parking lot and drive away.

Years later, the same thing may happen to him, and he thinks, "Karma!" as some sort of Divine retribution for his actions in the past. It is karma, but the behavior that originated the lesson is unimportant. It is not <u>what</u> happens that is the lesson; it's <u>how</u> we relate to it that contains the lesson. Do we react from ego or do we accept with love? Awareness, choice, and purposeful action and thought are the steps to access the love that is always there.

8. We create our lives.
While it is true that we are not alone, we are also independent. We have choice, we have free will, and we are supreme manifestors. When I began to awaken I would pray to God to use me as an instrument of Its Will. The deeper I immersed myself, letting go of ego and releasing karma, the more determined I was that my life would henceforth be of service and dedication to the Light. I kept asking – and kept waiting. No signs appeared, no revelations sprang forward in my thoughts, and no dreams instructed me in the "right" way of my path. I was frustrated. I was a willing volunteer to do whatever I was called upon to do: feed the poor, dig latrines in Sri Lanka, milk goats in central Africa, whatever. I waited and waited.

Sure, I knew the essence of my contract, inspiration, but what did it <u>mean</u>? Being a linear, logical, left brain type, meaning carried great importance. How was my essence to be expressed? I did not have a clue. "Come on, God, give me a hint. You know, like a book falling open to something significant, or a coffee stain on a map, or overhearing a chance conversation. Just let me know. I'm a resourceful type; I'll figure it out given a clue or two. Please!" Nothing.

In May 2000, I underwent a five-day fast in the Anza Borrego desert of southern California. On day five, I experienced vision and revelation. Part of the revelation had to do with our being the creators of our own lives. In my experience that day, I asked God once more what It wanted me to do. I figured that God would be in a great frame of mind to tell me, seeing as how I had gone through such deprivation for the last 100 plus hours. What I received as the answer to that question came as a great surprise.

God said, in effect, "It's up to you pal. You are the creator, you are the manifestor, Spirit is here to assist and lend a hand, not to dictate. We do sets and lighting. You are the author, director, and the star of the story of your life. Sorry. I know it is not what you wanted, but it is <u>the</u> answer. What else would you like to know?"

As I integrated the entire experience of the fast over the next few days and months, I started feeling lonely. I did not lose my sense of connection. But I did feel a sense of loss, for now I faced finding my own way and making my own decisions about how to express "inspiration." I knew that whatever I choose is okay, provided I choose with love and acceptance. In the matter of living my life, I was on my own. No divine index finger was going to appear and point me in the direction of my destiny. The upside of this knowledge came in the realization that whatever I do is in my highest and best interest **if** I act with gratitude and acceptance. There are no divine choices; it is a matter of choosing divinely.

9. There is nothing but energy.
Following the five-day desert fast, I soon received the first in a series of communications from Spirit called "Energetics." As I received this knowledge and transcribed it, I realized that I have responsibility for my life, that here was the knowledge with which to shape my life as I need it to be. I clearly received the message: "<u>Energy is everything. Understand this and all else is clear.</u>" Several months passed before I began to fully grasp those ten words.

All that is, has been, or ever will be manifest is nothing but energy. Human beings are of course nothing but energy by extrapolation. Our physicality is only one manifestation of the collection of energies defining an individual spirit that, although connected with all other energy, is a unique entity. As energetic bodies, we continuously release and receive various forms of energy. Our bodies demand nourishment, so we receive food, water, and oxygen, and we release physical movement, chemical interactions, electrical currents, and waste. That knowledge is neither new nor profound. There is much more.

We also release energy as emotions, thoughts, words, and actions. Anytime that we release energy, there is a return signature that causes like energies to be returned to us. In the matter of sustaining our bodies, when we release movement, create electrical currents, chemical interactions, and process waste, the return signatures cause us to seek those forms of energy from which we can create more movement, more electricity, and so forth. These releases and returns are automatic; we can, but mostly do not, have awareness about them. There is a principal of balance – when we release we must eventually receive to sustain balance.

In the matter of emotions, thoughts, words, and actions, balance must be maintained as well. When we release ego-based emotions, thoughts, words, and actions, we will receive energies in return that perpetuate that specific cycle of release and receive. If we release hate, then we will attract energies that will give us further opportunities to hate. This is the opportunity of karma endlessly repeating, **unless** we have the **awareness** to direct that love be returned to us, instead of more fear-based energy. Remember, awareness is the gateway to love was the sixth finding. Now you know why.

The principles of Energetics apply to more than karmic-based processes. They extend to manifesting what we desire materially as well as spiritually. Energetics is the mechanics of karma as well as of survival in our physical reality.

You have read *A Tao of God* and my findings in and around the experiences leading to the discovery and documentation of the 39 core chapters of the book. There are a few final points that I think are relevant.

First, please remember this is my experience and my personal truth. Different chapters and even the material within them will be discerned by different people in various ways; whatever works for you, take it and use it. Whatever doesn't, leave it behind.

Second, if you take nothing else with you, remember that **only you can heal you**. No one can do it for you. Others can support you and your process (whatever it may be) but they cannot heal you. Only you can go to your dark or shadow side and heal the wounds that caused you to think that you are less than who you truly are: a manifestation of God in human form; a spiritual being having a human experience.

Third, and last, remember that the key to beginning to walk your path directly toward harmony and fulfillment is **awareness** (Chapter 20). You have to know what is going on with and around you and the choices that are at hand, in order to use any tool, regardless of whose it is.

I wrote this at the end of the "Beginning" chapter:

Remember one essential "truth" as you explore *A Tao of God:*
Spiritual evolution is simple but not easy.
When you examine any "system" or "process" for healing and evolving yourself, including *A Tao of God,* if it does not seem simple, it is not for you.

If you found that *A Tao of God* is simple, then I encourage you to work with it, question every part of it, and what fits for you, take it on and try it out. **Experience** the **Knowledge** of *A Tao of God* and create your own **Understandings**. From there you can choose to **Transform** yourself as you so need. I honor you for being in action in the matter of your own evolution.

If *A Tao of God* does not fit your needs, then I urge you to look elsewhere, find other systems or processes for healing, and test them. I honor you for being in action in the matter of your own evolution.

I wish you the best in whatever you do with this material. It is my honor to present it to you.

Namasté - *I salute the highest in you.*
Ron McCray

Idyllwild, California
2003
www.turtlewheel.com

∞

ISBN 141200387-3

9 781412 003872